# THE PROTECTIVE TARIFF
# IN CANADA'S DEVELOPMENT

# THE PROTECTIVE TARIFF
# IN CANADA'S DEVELOPMENT

EIGHT ESSAYS ON

Trade and Tariffs When Factors Move

WITH SPECIAL REFERENCE TO

Canadian Protectionism 1870–1955

## J. H. DALES

UNIVERSITY OF TORONTO PRESS

# Preface

It sometimes happens that an author, in introducing a collection of his essays, feels obliged to convince prospective readers that there *is* a consistent line of thought running throughout the volume that serves to unify what at first sight may appear to be a very mixed bag. In this book, however, the unifying theme is hard to avoid, not hard to detect. True, its chapters began as separate essays written at various times over the past four years, and although they have been integrated, reorganized, and rewritten—some of them several times—they retain much of their original character. Nevertheless, though they are not sequential steps in a single argument, the eight chapters in the volume constitute a set of associated essays, each of which leads up to the same theme from a different angle. Six of them are published here for the first time. Chapter 2 is reprinted with only minor typographical changes from the *Canadian Journal of Economics and Political Science*, vol. XXX, no. 4 (November, 1964). The first part of Chapter 7 is a reprinting of the first part of my article "Some Historical and Theoretical Comment on Canada's National Policies" that originally appeared in the *Queen's Quarterly*, vol. LXXI, no. 3 (Autumn, 1964); the last part of the chapter was written for the present volume. (In footnote 5 of the original article my comments on a paper by D. J. Daly were incorrect; what I hope is a correct reporting of his findings is given in footnote 8 of chapter 6.)

Many perceptive readers and critics of earlier versions of the present essays have led me to revise and improve my arguments, and to all of them I express my deep gratitude. I owe especially large debts for time and enlightenment to my colleagues H. A. J. Green, H. C. Eastman, and D. M. Nowlan at the University of Toronto, to J. C. Weldon of McGill University, and to H. G. Johnson of the University of Chicago. They have helped me enormously with particular points and particular chapters, and I am proud to have learned from them. I do not, however, expect any of them to agree with all the propositions put forward in the book, and I want to make it perfectly clear that none of them bears any responsibility for either the general tenor of my argument or its main conclusions.

I wish to thank the University of Toronto Press and the Social Science Research Council of Canada for their financial support of this volume. My last word is for the man with the last word; I am most grateful to R. I. K. Davidson for his helpful, shrewd, and expeditious editing. (He will probably change *that* sentence too!)*

*Toronto, June, 1966*                                                J.H.D.

*Not so! R.I.K.D.

# Contents

# Introduction

My interest in the economic effects of the Canadian tariff was first aroused by the blank disagreement between treatises on trade theory, which assure us that a protective tariff is almost always a "bad thing," and many writings on the economic history of Canada which assure us that the Canadian tariff, adopted in 1879 under the name of the National Policy, has been a "very good thing." In the course of trying to sort out this disagreement I have come to be very dissatisfied both with existing interpretations of the role played by the National Policy in Canadian economic development and with the existing theory of international trade, a rather inbred branch of economics where logical purity seems to have been pursued for its own sake and at an increasing cost in terms of economic relevance. I have tried in what follows to modify this theory in several respects with an eye to making it at once more general and more relevant to the problems of historical interpretation and policy formation. One result of the modifications is to support the contention of Canadian historians that the National Policy has enlarged the population and national income of Canada; but, so far as income per person is concerned, the main result of the revision is to add several new charges to the standard textbook indictment of protective tariffs. Moreover, the empirical essays point to the conclusion that the economic evils of protectionism have been particularly virulent in Canada.

The sixth essay in this volume was the first to be written and was the progenitor of all the others. In preparing it I

1

in the country at the existing money wage rate. This over-simplification of reality has at least as much to recommend it as its alternative. It is certainly more realistic, since the volume of immigration into a country is closely correlated with the degree of "prosperity" in the country (immigration regulations practically ensure such a correlation!); and it is not obviously inferior as a "behavioural" hypothesis, since people are most likely to emigrate when they know that there are jobs awaiting them at their destination than when they know that unemployment exists in the country where they will disembark. But consider the analytical difference. A tariff will now *increase* a country's population since it will create new job opportunities in the protected industries, thus encouraging immigration, and will of course do nothing to encourage emigration by creating new job opportunities in other countries.

Still, the argument for a reduced per capita income in the "migration function" is not without force, and the effect of the tariff in leading to emigration from Canada as a result of its downward pressure on the standard of living must be reckoned with. The net balance of tariff-induced emigration *and* immigration is discussed more fully in chapter 2 and again in chapter 6. In general it seems that, in the past at any rate, Canada has had no trouble in attracting enough immigrants *both* to replace the emigrants who have left the country because of the tariff *and* to provide (along with natural increase) a labour force for the expansion of our protected manufacturing industries. I was recently encouraged to find that Professor John Porter, working on an entirely different problem, had come to a view of the roles played by immigration and emigration in Canada's social and political development that seems roughly to complement my own views of their relationship to our economic development.[3] What is painfully clear, in any event, is that much more thought needs to be devoted to the interactions between the very large flows of people to and from Canada on the one hand and various aspects of Canadian development on the other.

[3]John Porter, *The Vertical Mosaic* (Toronto, 1965), chap. 2.

4

The third essay, the last of the theoretical trio, could perhaps be characterized as "tedious." If so, it derives this quality from the complexity of the analysis rather than from the problem under discussion, which I must admit I find quite fascinating. The question is how the passage of economic time, marked off by changes in tastes and technologies, affects the protection actually provided by a tariff structure that is left unchanged through time. Does its economic effectiveness wither away, remain unchanged, or become greater as the decades unfold? I was made aware of the importance of this sort of question by the late W. E. G. Salter's brilliant book on *Productivity and Technical Change.*[4] In it he asked, not how a single innovation changed an industry's equilibrium from one point in time to another point in time, but how a *flow of innovations* through time affected the equilibrium of an industry *through* time. I ask how the flow of changing tastes and technologies through time, impinging on an unchanging tariff, affects the secular development of an economy. Although my analysis of this problem is, I know, seriously incomplete, it does show clearly that the immediate effects of *introducing* a policy—a tariff, or an income tax, or a social security policy—are not a satisfactory guide to the effects, ten or twenty years later, of the law that enshrines that policy. Whatever one government intended to do by introducing a tariff, something different is quite likely to result under its successors who maintain it. The complexity of the questions raised, if not answered, in chapter 3 makes one doubt whether governments that retain unchanged a tariff structure originally adopted long ago have the foggiest idea of what they are doing to the contemporary economy and the contemporary electorate. But despite the complexity of the problem I have attempted to indicate the probable effects of maintaining a constant tariff in a changing world. It will come as no surprise that an avowed free-trader has been able to wring from the analysis several new charges to add to his indictment of protectionism.

4Cambridge, 1960. See esp. pp. 4–6.

The three essays in Part II of the volume are for economic historians and policy-makers; they are factual, historical studies that seek to throw light on Canadian economic development by a careful comparison of various economic trends in Canada with the corresponding trends in the United States. Chapter 4 is a rather self-conscious attempt to justify the method of "comparative history" in general and my own Canadian : American comparison in particular. Methodology is rarely exciting reading, but the chapter is a necessary explanation of the comparison that underlies the argument in chapters 5 and 6.

One of the main purposes of chapter 4 is to demonstrate by a rather rough, but to my mind wholly convincing, syllogism that the American tariff, despite its intent, has not in fact protected American manufacturing; and that American manufacturing experience therefore provides a "free trade" standard, or control, against which to compare Canadian manufacturing experience. The point is an important one because, historically, the most persuasive argument for protectionism in Canada is the observation that the United States became the strongest economic power in the world under a protectionist policy. True. But the observation provides no justification for the conclusion that American economic pre-eminence *resulted from* the American tariff. The explanation of American success obviously *may* lie elsewhere; I argue that it *must* lie elsewhere, and that it is not astonishing that Canada, though emulating American tariff policy, has not matched American economic performance. But mere reason has seldom discredited a popular theory, and Canadians to this day retain a touching faith in protectionism as a royal road to riches. One is reminded of the Stephen Leacock character who became convinced, from wide reading on the lives of successful men, that every leading banker had begun his career by "hitting town with only a nickel in his pocket," and who thereupon reduced his assets to five cents and attempted to repeat the experiment—with dispiriting results.

Chapter 5 proceeds rather shakily—but I hope reasonably

convincingly—to the conclusion that the Canadian tariff, unlike the American, has done what it was intended to do: to protect from world competition Canadian manufacturers who produce at costs above world costs. Those who cannot accept the "direct" proof of this proposition in chapter 5 will at least agree that the "conclusion" of that chapter, when reduced to the status of a "hypothesis," is "not inconsistent with" the data presented in chapter 6. It is pretty tough to "prove" anything in an age that accepts (I think rightly) the ethic that only disproof is scientifically respectable. But there is still persuasion!

Chapter 6 presents the data that, as noted earlier, posed the problem that led to all the other essays in this volume. I hate to think of how many hours I have stared at the chart in that chapter, seeking to read its meaning; and of how many times I thought I had the answer, only to have it shot full of holes by one or another of my colleagues in economic theory. Economic history is not worth writing unless its arguments are theoretically sound—or unless they can be *made* theoretically sound, which may require the theory to be modified and in the process, one hopes, improved. There is still a great gulf between economic theory and economic history, partly, I think, because theorists abhor time and change and historians make their livings by studying them, and partly because I am convinced that theorists and historians play different games. Economic theorists are concerned with making the best use of *given* resources (owned by a household, a firm, or a nation) while historians, as a result of their interest in time and change, tend to become primarily concerned with the causes of the *growth* of resources and to write off problems relating to the efficient use of *given* resources as problems in "the second order of smalls." The conclusions I arrive at in chapter 6 (and in the volume as a whole) illustrate what I mean: the tariff increases GNP in Canada by increasing the resources of labour and capital domiciled in Canada—which is why historians think it is a "good thing"; at the same time it reduces GNP per capita in Canada by reducing the efficiency of the economy—which is why theorists condemn it as a "bad thing."

7

I must say that I think the theorists have the better position to defend. While the study of the accretion of resources to an economy is of obvious importance, the trouble with the historian's game is that there is nothing to maximize or minimize, and therefore no basis for ending the game and declaring a winner; there is no end, short of world conquest, to the accumulation of resources within national borders. On the other hand the theorists should not remain content to defend an impregnable position. The household, the firm, and the nation *are* interested in increasing their resources as well as in making the most of their existing resources; yet while economic theory has something to say about the economic size of firms, it is largely silent on what determines the equilibrium size of households and nations. There is a fascinating gulf between economic history and economic theory, and I cannot see why a joint attempt to bridge it should jeopardize the identity of either work-party.

## III

Throughout Part II of this volume I have tried to abide by the methodological rules that prevent my claiming to have proved anything and confine me to the circumlocution that my evidence does not seem to disprove my thesis, but in chapter 6 the strain begins to show and I tend to slide from science into rhetoric. In Part III of the volume I think I have achieved almost complete freedom from scientific inhibitions, though I hope I have not confused freedom with licence. Chapter 7 was written originally as a piece of historical debunkery, which is to say that it was, and is, a serious expression of personal views on the subject. Chapter 8 is a brazen attempt to persuade the Economic Council of Canada, and anyone else who will listen, that arguments based on "economies of scale" are, more often than not, dangerous economic nonsense.

# I

# 1

# Comparative Advantage and Factor Mobility

All trade, we may say, depends on comparative advantage.[1] But on what does comparative advantage depend? Two broad answers to this question are given in the literature: an assumption of different production functions for the same commodity in different regions; and an assumption of different ratios of factor endowments (supplies) in different regions.[2] The combination of either of these assumptions with the standard assumption of interregional factor immobility provides a

[1]Cases of "absolute advantage" may be considered cases of infinite comparative advantage. Nevertheless the statement in the text implies certain limitations on the definition of trade that need explicit mention. The concept of comparative advantage applies only to the production of commodities, meaning thereby both goods and "commodity services"; trade therefore relates only to an exchange of commodities for commodities. Exchanges of "factor services" for commodities (e.g., goods exports to cover interest payments) or of factor services for factor services (e.g., rent receipts for interest payments) or of commodities for transfer payments (e.g., goods imports for receipt of foreign aid) or of commodities against factor supplies (e.g., an import of goods against an import of capital) are not trade. Such exchanges enter into a balance of payment, but none involves trade based on comparative advantage. Similarly, the import of goods into a dormitory suburb to balance the outflow of labour services is exchange, and satisfies a balance of payments constraint, but it is not trade. The distinction between "exchange" and "trade based on comparative advantage" is unimportant in standard trade theory because factors are normally considered immobile; when, in special cases, the immobility assumption is relaxed, factor movements are often assumed rather than explained, as in the literature on "hot money" capital movements, unilateral transfers, immigrants' remittances, and so on.
[2]See J. Bhagwati, "The Pure Theory of International Trade," *Economic Journal*, March, 1964, pp. 1–84, esp. sec. I, pp. 4–29.

sufficient—indeed, a more than sufficient—condition for comparative advantage.

# I

The older of the two current explanations of comparative advantage—here referred to as the classical view—is based on the assumption that production of the same commodity is subject to different production functions in different regions. Two reasons why production functions should differ regionally may be advanced. It may be claimed that units of the factors of production themselves differ between regions, so that, for example, a unit of labour in Europe is fundamentally different, in some qualitative sense, from a unit of labour in America. I make no use of this argument; it has no logical advantage over its alternative, and has the serious disadvantage of leading eventually to the treacherous problem of translating natural units of factors into equivalent efficiency units.

I assume, therefore, that units of factors are qualitatively identical in different regions. Production functions, which are here defined to include *only* paid inputs, may nevertheless differ between regions because the "environment of production" differs between regions. The environment of production is taken to refer to features of both the physical and social environment—such things as climate and topography on the one hand, and social customs and governmental policies on the other—which in any given region affect some production activities favourably, and others unfavourably. An assumption of different production functions in different regions does not provide a sufficient condition for comparative advantage. Roughly speaking, it would lead either to trade based solely on "absolute advantage" (if England can produce cloth more cheaply than Portugal, and Portugal can produce wine more cheaply than England, all weavers would move to England and all wine-makers to Portugal) or to no trade at all (if Portugal can produce both cloth and wine more cheaply than England everyone would move to Portugal). These "predictions," of course, are patently at odds with observations of real world trade, and to prevent their emerging from the argument it is necessary to add to the assumption of different production functions an assumption that imposes restrictions on the movement of factors from one region to another. Ricardo assumed complete immobility of all factors between regions, and this assumption has been employed in trade theory ever since. Taken together, the production function assumption and the immobility assumption provide a set of sufficient conditions for *comparative* advantage, and thus for trade between two countries even when one of them can produce both commodities more cheaply than the other. The "classical" position, in brief, assumes production functions to differ between countries, but places no restriction on "factor proportions"—comparative advantage would exist even if the proportions of (paid) factors were identical in all countries.

What we shall call the "modern" theory of comparative advantage shows that the mirror opposites of the classical assumptions also provide sufficient conditions for trade. The modern theory assumes that factor proportions differ between countries, but places no restriction on production functions—comparative advantage would exist even if production functions were identical in all countries. To the factor proportions assumption is added the Ricardian assumption about factor immobility, and the result is again a set of sufficient conditions for comparative advantage. Both approaches, it will be noted, make use of the Ricardian immobility assumption; it is this assumption, I shall argue, that makes the set of sufficient conditions for comparative advantage stronger than it needs to be in both the classical and modern approaches to the topic.

The weaker assumption about production employed by the modern approach to comparative advantage has led to notable extensions of trade theory, and through these to an improved understanding of the complex nature of comparative advantage itself. The relative money costs of production of a particular commodity in different regions are seen to depend in the first instance on the ratios of factor prices in the different

13

regions; but, beyond that, factor price ratios in any one region are themselves seen to depend partly on the ratios of factor supplies in that region and partly on the total pattern of output in the region, for on this pattern depends the configuration of factor demands. Comparative advantage, then, like everything else in economics, turns out to be the solution to a complex system of simultaneous equations; it is the end result of the interaction of all variables in the economies of all regions. It is mainly a matter of convention that in all this flux economists choose as an assumed rigidity on which to base further argument the statement that ratios of factor supplies are (a) fixed in each region, and (b) different in different regions; and it is only in this sense that comparative advantage may be said to depend on different ratios of factor endowments in different regions. Logically, any other assumed fixity would serve as well; it is recognized, for example, that regional differences in the configurations of tastes, even with identical patterns of factor endowments, would also (together with the factor immobility assumption) provide a sufficient basis for comparative advantage.

The assumption of fixed factor endowments is not, of course, a purely arbitrary convention; supplies of those factors of production known collectively as "land" *are* fixed by Nature, and it is a common observation that even inherently movable factors of production seldom move perfectly freely between regions. But it is an equally common observation that some factors of production *do* flow across regional frontiers in large volumes and change their "residence" either temporarily or permanently. These flows presumably tend to reduce the inequality of factor-supply ratios in different regions, and thus to erode comparative advantage. Similarly, interregional movements of people presumably tend to reduce regional differences in tastes, and thus to erode this source of comparative advantage. It is to prevent this erosion and also to avoid the necessity of dealing simultaneously with two different ranges of problems—goods movements and factor movements—that trade theory outdoes Nature by assuming *all* factors of production to be *completely* immobile between

14

regions. In this sense, the postulate of comparative advantage, though not entirely dependent on the immobility assumption, is certainly protected by that assumption. The question is whether the assumption is not overly protective. I shall argue that it is, and that it needlessly inhibits an extension of present trade theory to explain factor movements as well as goods movements.

## II

The immobility assumption of trade theory can be greatly weakened without destroying comparative advantage. All that is required for trade is sufficient immobility to ensure that factor-supply ratios in different regions cannot be equalized. Let us begin by considering two extreme cases of mobility. Imagine that *all* factors are completely mobile. Assume also that it is always less costly to move a unit of a factor once than to pay for repeated movements of the goods produced by that unit, so that whenever there is a choice of moving goods or moving factors the factors will move. Given these assumptions (which will be discussed more fully below) it is obvious that there will be no trade, because factors will move around until factor proportions are the same in all regions. If all factors save one were assumed to be perfectly mobile the same conclusion would apply; the mobile factors would adjust to the immobile factor until factor proportions were identical in every region. Again there would be no comparative advantage and no trade.

The situation changes dramatically if we now assume *two* immobile factors (or even two factors each of which is less than perfectly mobile) to be present in different regions in different proportions. No amount of reshuffling of mobile factors can now equalize factor-supply ratios in different regions. Accordingly, what we might call the Rule of Two—the assumption that a minimum of two less than perfectly mobile factors of production are present in different proportions in different regions—provides a necessary and sufficient

15

condition for comparative advantage, and thus for trade. The normal assumption in trade theory that all factors are completely immobile interregionally is unnecessarily strong, and therefore inelegant.

Two features of the above argument require discussion. The assumption that factor movements will always be preferred to goods movements whenever there is a choice between them is logical artifice. Its functions in the above argument is to render determinate what would otherwise be an indeterminate mixture of goods movements and factor movements.[3] It relates only to cases where factors are considered to be *perfectly* mobile, and since I make little use of such cases in the rest of the essay its realism need not be justified at length. The rationale of the assumption is simply that it seems reasonable to suppose that the discounted present value of the costs of transporting the lifetime output of a unit of a factor of production from $A$ to $B$ will be greater than the costs of moving the factor from $A$ to $B$; and that transport costs will accordingly be minimized by moving the factor rather than its output. In the real world, of course, this sort of "either–or" situation is rare, and the relevant question is almost always *how much* factor movement is involved either in the maintenance of, or the restoration of, an economic equilibrium. Otherwise expressed, the relevant question is normally not *whether* a factor is mobile but *how* mobile it is.

The concept of (geographic) mobility, as used in economic literature, is badly in need of semantic attention. It is commonly used in three distinct senses: (1) movability, the physical and legal possibility of moving or being moved; (2) willingness to move; and (3) movement, a magnitude that can be quantified and measured. It is less important, for our purposes, to distinguish between the first and second senses than to separate them clearly and unambiguously from the third. Imagine a diagram where some "incentive to move" is measured along the $y$ axis and the amount of movement is measured along the $x$ axis. Perfect immobility, whether as a

[3]R. E. Caves, *Trade and Economic Structure* (Cambridge, Mass., 1960), pp. 122–3.

result of immovability or of complete unwillingness to move regardless of the incentive to do so, would be depicted as a vertical line coincident with the $y$ axis. Perfect mobility, implying that any incentive to move would call forth whatever amount of movement was required to remove the incentive, would be represented by a horizontal line coincident with the $x$ axis. All cases of imperfect mobility would then be represented by upward sloping curves of different positions and elasticities. Empirically, of course, mobility is likely to display a discouragingly large amount of variability; different units of a factor no doubt vary markedly in mobility, and the average mobility displayed by regional aggregates of a given factor probably differs greatly in different regions at any one time, and at different times in any one region. What is important for our purposes, however, is the well known difference in mobility as between factors: at one end of the spectrum are those factors, collectively referred to as land, that are completely immobile because immovable; at the other extreme lies capital, some subdivisions of which may approach perfect mobility; in between is labour, which in different groupings displays a very wide range of mobilities.

I have so far been careful to refer vaguely to *some* incentive to move. Before the concept of mobility could be elaborated into a theory of factor movements the precise incentive, or combination of incentives, would have to be specified. It is no part of my present purpose to take up this problem, but one comment seems appropriate in order to emphasize its importance. The easy hypothesis that factor migration is a simple function of interregional differences in a factor's real income seems too cavalier. Interregional differences in employment opportunities, measured by differences in excess demand for the factor at *existing* money incomes, has at least an equal claim to attention.[4] In particular cases, the two hypo-

[4]The mobility of a movable factor, for example labour, is certainly a function of transfer costs, among other things, and transfer costs must be construed to include the value of foregone earnings over the period "from job to job." This item will obviously be much higher when there is unemployment in the country of destination and full employment in the country of origin than it would be if the reverse were the case.

theses may lead to entirely different results: for example, in an inflation where money wages lag, the real-income differential hypothesis would indicate net emigration, while the money–excess demand hypothesis would produce net immigration. It is clearly possible, in other words, for a region to experience *increasing* immigration in combination with a *falling* real wage, provided only that its real wage remains higher than the real wage in the region whence the immigrants come. Careful empirical work is needed in order to produce a defensible "migration function." A sophisticated theory of factor migration seems well worth developing as an important part of economics in its own right, quite apart from its close connection with trade theory developed under an assumption of (imperfect) factor mobility.[5]

### III

By using the "differential mobility" theory of comparative advantage the simultaneous determination of factor movements and goods movements becomes possible. It is only the uncompromising factor-immobility assumption that prevents an extension of standard trade theory to explain factor movements; once it is recognized that only *two* imperfectly mobile factors, present in different proportions in different regions, need be assumed in order to ensure trade, it becomes possible to provide a unified explanation of the interregional movement of both goods and factors. To put the matter another way, the specification of "factor-migration" functions should make it possible to integrate trade theory and location theory,

[5]Units of a given regional supply of a given factor are presumed to be identical only with respect to their productive capability. Regional supplies of labour and entrepreneurship may differ markedly in the important respect of their preferences for place of residence, which will be a major determinant of their mobility. A preference for a particular region of residence may reflect, amongst other things, the habits of work in the region (relevant to the factor's valuation of leisure in terms of income) and the habits of consumption in the region (relevant to the factor's pattern of tastes); in the present essay, however, we assume tastes, including the valuation of leisure, to be the same in all regions.

18

that woefully weak and neglected subject that is nevertheless the only branch of economics that concerns itself with the role of factor movements in interregional equilibrium.

A unified explanation of both goods movements and factor movements will, of course, require a change in the specifications of the standard trade model.[6] Two-factor models in which both factors are perfectly immobile generate trade without factor movements. Two-factor models in which both factors are imperfectly mobile, or in which one is perfectly immobile and the other imperfectly immobile, will generate factor movements without destroying trade. But a two-factor model in which one factor is completely mobile and the other completely immobile will produce only factor movement; trade will be destroyed.[7] If mobility is taken to be an all-or-nothing proposition at least a three-factor model must be used—two immobile factors to produce trade and one mobile factor to produce factor movement. A completely general, $n$-factor model could assume different mobilities, ranging in magnitude from infinity to zero, for different factors. So long as the Rule of Two is met the model will produce trade, and

[6]Models already exist in which factor supplies are taken to be a function of trade; trade may raise a factor's price and call forth an additional "supply" of that factor from a given "endowment." Relevant literature is reviewed in Caves, *Trade and Economic Structure*, pp. 101–10, and Caves points out that the argument can be applied to cases where the variation in factor supply results from interregional migration of the factor (p. 109). But in fact the argument has *not* been consistently applied to such cases, and a theory of interregional factor migration can scarcely be said to exist in the theoretical literature.

[7]Thus a two-factor model in which labour is assumed to be completely immobile and capital completely mobile will not produce trade under our assumption that factor movements will always be preferred to goods movements. In such a model capital would move until factor proportions were identical in the two regions. R. A. Mundell works with precisely this model in his article, "International Trade and Factor Mobility," in the *American Economic Review*, June, 1957, pp. 321–35. He concludes that trade will be eliminated (p. 325). (There remains an export of goods to service the imported capital—capitalists do not move with their capital—but this is of course an exchange of goods against factor services. It is not trade, for it is not an exchange of goods against goods resulting from comparative advantage. See n. 1 above. The equilibrium capital import is also a neutral equilibrium only, for on p. 325 it is stated that other amounts of capital imports "would be consistent" with equilibrium.) Mundell's model is therefore inconsistent with trade and can scarcely be called a trade model.

19

so long as complete immobility of all factors is *not* assumed it will also generate factor movements.

The chief usefulness of a differential mobility view of comparative advantage lies in the area of intraregional or "domestic" trade, where existing trade theory is weakest. The unnecessarily strong factor-immobility assumption of standard trade theory is not unduly debilitating when the theory is applied to *international* trade, where major obstacles to factor mobility undoubtedly exist; but it becomes ridiculous when applied to trade within a nation, since one of the underlying purposes of a nation state is presumably to provide for free movement of factors within its borders. In a strictly literal sense, trade theory has nothing whatever to say about "domestic" or intra-unit trade; if international trade theory is applied to trade between regions within a nation, we have no theory of intraregional trade; if to provinces within a region we have no theory of intra-provincial trade; and so on. Even when applied to large regions within a nation, trade theory becomes artificial and unconvincing. If regional factor supplies may be considered fixed (perfectly immobile) at any one moment of time, they cannot reasonably be assumed to remain so for very many moments. Factor movements as well as goods movements must surely be regarded as an essential part of the mechanism that produces interregional equilibrium.

But, of course, if one abandons trade theory, and jumps to the opposite extreme by assuming that *all* factors are perfectly mobile within a nation, everything is lost, for as was shown in section II this assumption leads to the conclusion that domestic trade does not exist! The differential-mobility view of comparative advantage, by producing models that explain both factor movements and goods movements, leads naturally to a theory of domestic commerce and interregional equilibrium.[8] It also provides a symmetrical explanation of international equilibrium on the one hand and interregional

[8]B. Ohlin's claim to have done precisely this in his *Interregional and International Trade* (Cambridge, Mass., 1933) is not without foundation. He certainly assumed implicitly the sort of "differential-mobility" view of comparative advantage recommended here. He allowed factor movements, so he did not assume complete interregional immobility of factors; he did not assume complete mobility of all factors because had he done so the result

(intranational) equilibrium on the other, thereby avoiding the sharp incongruity of assumption in existing trade theory where factors are assumed to be completely immobile between geographical units and, at least by implication, completely mobile within geographical units.[9]

## IV

In every important economic assumption there lies embedded a conclusion that has some implication for policy; what is amazing is that the policy implication often gains political currency and is used by men who have no clear understanding of its genesis. Assumptions about comparative advantage provide good examples. In the classical view, comparative advantage, and therefore the direction and composition of trade, depends ultimately on "environment"; by implication, governments are for the most part powerless to affect their trading relationships since most aspects of the environment— geography, climate, culture, and social customs—are well beyond their control, except perhaps in the *very* long run. And so long as this approach to comparative advantage dominated the field, governments *did* seem to take a fatalistic view of trade; comparative advantage, like technology and tastes, was something to be adjusted to, not adjusted.

By contrast, the "modern" view makes comparative advantage depend primarily on the relative supplies of factors of production that are domiciled within the political boundaries of a region. Rightly or wrongly, governments commonly reject the immobility assumption of trade theory and attempt to

---

of his model would have been either no trade or an indeterminate combination of factor movements and goods movements. Under our assumption that factor movements will always be preferred to goods movements the solution would have been determinate at zero trade. By failing to specify mobilities Ohlin was unable to relate factor movements to income differentials or some other "incentive to move"; he was thus unable to determine from his model the equilibrium amount of factor movement and unable to show the precise mixture of factor movements and trade that produced interregional economic equilibrium.

[9]Trade theorists commonly make this assumption explicit when they are engaged in refuting protectionist arguments based on intranational immobilities of factors.

21

influence the relative factor supplies under their control by any number of policies ranging from forced savings and interest rate policies, through subsidies for research and education to immigration policies. Indeed if governments *can* influence their relative factor supplies they can, according to modern theory, affect the pattern of their comparative advantages. In the extreme case a government could choose any set of comparative advantages it wished, and accordingly achieve any pattern of trade it wished. Whether mere coincidence or not, increasing acceptance of the modern assumption about comparative advantage in academic circles has been accompanied by a rise of government interest, especially in new countries and semi-industrialized young countries, in trade *policies*, frequently in the form of developmental strategies that are intended to alter in a fundamental way a country's position in the world economy.

The differential-mobility view of comparative advantage presented in this essay is something of a compromise between the classical and modern views. It accepts the latter's position that production functions are the same in all countries. But it insists that different factors, and even different regional supplies of the same factor, may have different degrees of mobility, and that the environment stressed by the classical view may have much to do with factor mobility, hence with factor proportions, and hence with trade. Thus the policy implications of the differential-mobility view also represent a compromise between the policy implications of the classical and modern views. Classical comparative advantage emphasizes "land"—natural resources and by extension all features of the natural environment—as playing a dominant role in trade; it no doubt overemphasizes this role and discounts too heavily the ability of a government, through its economic policies, to affect a region's factor proportions and thus its trade. But surely the modern view is unbalanced in the other direction; to minimize the role of natural resources and "environment" in production, and to write production functions solely in terms of $L$ and $K$, two factors that everyone knows to be mobile, perhaps serves to encourage the vulgar view that anything can be economically produced anywhere.

It is in domestic affairs, specifically in the burgeoning field of "regional economic policy" and among the proponents of policies of "moving jobs to people," that various versions of the "anything-anywhere" thesis are most frequently encountered. The strong immobility assumption of trade theory has perhaps prevented trade theorists from showing clearly that interregional equilibrium, especially within a nation, depends on a particular pattern of factor distribution as well as on a particular pattern of trade; by default the field has been left to location theorists who have a weak sense of comparative advantage and who write loosely of "footloose" industries.[10] A differential-mobility view of comparative advantage, by encouraging the use of models that would show equilibrium positions for both interregional trade and regional factor supplies, would have the wholly desirable side-effect of warning governments that neither equilibrium can be violated without economic penalty.

APPENDIX I

THE CANADA–UNITED STATES AUTOMOTIVE AGREEMENT

A brief comment on the recent Canadian-American automobile agreement will serve to illustrate some of the points made in this chapter, and even to extend the argument somewhat. In particular the pact seems to me to be a prime example of how policy reflects hidden assumptions about production costs and the nature of comparative advantage. The assumptions in this case are so plausible, so obviously

---

[10]This tendency in modern thought derives from the emphasis given to manufacturing and service industries, apparently based largely on the mobile factors of labour and capital, as contrasted with the emphasis given to agriculture and therefore to "land," the immobile factor *par excellence*, in classical economics. But the fact that manufacturing and service industries use processed materials ("working capital") rather than natural resources does not justify the conclusion that such industries are footloose. There are chain relationships in production between all firms, as input-output tables illustrate. It may be suggested that there are similar (though not the same) chain relationships in location; firms are not only linked in an output sense through quantities of inputs but also in a locational sense through the mobilities of inputs. I doubt that a perfectly footloose industry exists. The electronics industry is often said to be footloose because it locates near a university. Any university? Is any university mobile? Where do universities locate? If near centres of population, and if centres of population are located near agricultural land, then electronics industries are located on the basis of soil fertility.

"right," that they challenge the credibility of the quite different views about production, comparative advantage, and the limitations of policy that have been advanced in this chapter.

In January, 1965, the Canadian government inaugurated an automobile policy which is based, essentially, on the assumption that it should be possible to produce automobiles as cheaply in Windsor as in Detroit, a few hundred yards to the west, across the international border. At first blush it seems senseless to challenge this assumption. Yet in order to accept it one would be forced to believe that the present importation of automobiles (here considered a homogeneous product) into Canada is not based on any comparative advantage of Detroit over Windsor in automobile production. Accordingly one would have to explain the trade in automobiles by one or more of the following arguments: (1) the initial location of the industry in Detroit rather than Windsor was a historical accident, and economies of scale, both of the firm and of the industry, tend to keep the industry where it originally located; (2) the industry would in fact be more economically located in Windsor, but uneconomic policies consciously pursued by American automobile manufacturers for nationalistic reasons, or perhaps as the result of entrepreneurial inertia, keep the industry in Detroit; (3) economies of scale are so large in the automotive industries that costs of production are determined primarily by the size of national market served, and Detroit's advantage over Windsor is purely a market advantage.

The Canadian government appears to rest its case on the last two arguments. It attaches especial importance to the third argument, and the automobile accord of January, 1965, between Canada and the United States was designed to remove the market obstacle to Canadian automobile production. One of the terms of the international agreement is that the United States will remove its small tariff (6½ per cent on automobiles and 8½ per cent on parts) against imports of Canadian automobiles and parts; the large American market, it is said, will thereby be "made available" to the Canadian industry. The government has also indicated that it will be vigilant in pointing out to American automobile entrepreneurs their failures as profit-maximizers, in the hope that the second argument noted above may be reduced in force, if not entirely eliminated.[11] These things having been

---

[11]See the Minister's introductory statement on the agreement in a news release by the Department of Industry, January 15, 1965. "The difference in size and financial strength of the respective industries of Canada and the United States, the pattern of ownership and control, the deeply imbedded habits and customs prevailing in the industry and the many other institutional impediments to trade have all been taken into account in formulating the new program. These factors would make it difficult for the Canadian industry to compete on a fair and equitable basis even with the removal of United States tariffs and other formal barriers." (p. 6) In apparent reference to this sentiment, the Minister adds that when the agreement is reviewed in 1968: "In particular, Canada will wish to be assured that institutional barriers now limiting Canadian producton and trade have been eliminated or substantially reduced. . . ." (p. 8)

done, the Canadian government apparently believes that there is now no reason why the automotive industries should not grow more rapidly in Canada than in the United States. (Just to be on the safe side, though, the government has exacted a "guarantee" from each firm in the industry that this will happen.) The goal, we are led to believe, is that Canada should produce as many automobiles as it consumes, the suggestion being that Canada would then have a fair share of the market. To the medieval theologians' concept of the just price the Canadian government has added the concept of the just output.[12]

The production conditions we assume contradict the assumption on which this modern "theology" of trade is based. Our assumption provides that in general there will necessarily be a difference in the cost of producing automobiles in Detroit and in Windsor, even if there is complete free trade in all commodities between Canada and the United States. In arguing this proposition it is necessary to keep in mind that the concept of "per unit cost of production" is perhaps the most ambiguous concept in the lexicon of popular economics, and that scientific usage demands that the *output* at which any per unit cost applies must be specified. What our proposition asserts is that, except in circumstances that are so special that they may be ignored, the per unit costs of producing automobiles in Detroit and Windsor cannot be the same at all levels of output. They may be higher in one city than the other at all levels of output, or higher in one city than the other at some outputs and lower at others, but they cannot be the same in both cities at the same levels of output over the whole range of relevant outputs.

We may discuss this proposition by reference to one of the proudest achievements of trade theory, the factor-price equalization theorem. This theorem states that, given a long list of highly artificial assumptions, free trade will lead to the equalization of factor prices (and

---

[12]Among the special features of the agreement, the most important "is provided by the assurances of Canadian motor vehicle manufacturers to expand very considerably Canadian production over the next three and a half years. Whereas Canada now produces some 4.0 per cent of total North American automotive production, it consumes about 7.5 per cent. As a result of the new program, Canada should be producing a substantially larger share of total North American output by the time vehicles for the 1968 model year are on the road" (*ibid.*, pp. 7–8). It is apparently in reference to the excess of Canadian consumption over Canadian production that the Minister says that the agreement will allow the Canadian industry to gain "*a fair and equitable* share of the expanding North American market" (p. 2), is designed to overcome "institutional impediments" which would otherwise prevent the Canadian industry from competing "on a *fair and equitable* basis" (p. 6), and will be evaluated in 1968 on the basis of whether the Canadian industry then has "adequate opportunity to participate *fully and equitably* in the expanding North American market" (p. 8). Just for good measure the press summary that accompanied the news release said that the Canadian industry had given assurances that it would "participate *fully and equitably* in the expanding North American market" (p. 2). Italics added.

therefore the ratios of factor prices) between areas that are endowed with the same factors of production in different proportions and subject to identical production functions. This result derives from the fact that in equilibrium there will be *different* patterns of production in the two areas, i.e., in general, the output of any product will differ between the two areas. In brief, if the just price is achieved—equal factor prices in the two areas—the just output—identical patterns of output in the two areas—cannot be achieved; the just price is consistent *only* with one particular pattern of output, and will in general be inconsistent with any given specification of just output. The factor-price equalization theorem, viewed in this light, contains within itself a logically complete theory of the interregional location of industry. Its implication is that equalization of wage rates and interest rates between any two geographic areas—whether large or small, and whether in the same political jurisdiction or in different jurisdictions—depends on the areas' having *different* patterns of production, and therefore trading with one another in order that each may make good its deficiencies. The theorem shows, in brief, that economic efficiency requires that each region have a *particular* pattern of output, and therefore gives the lie to such easy assertions as "jobs should be moved to people," "most manufacturing industries are 'footloose,'" "it should be as cheap to produce automobiles in Windsor as in Detroit, or Montreal," and, in general, that "anything can be produced anywhere as economically as anywhere else." A government can pursue just-price policies designed to promote equal per capita incomes between different regions within its own country, in which case it must be willing to accept different production patterns in different regions; or it can pursue just-output policies designed to foster the same production patterns in different regions, in which case it must be willing to accept per capita income differentials between regions. The same applies, *pari passu*, to international differences in incomes and output patterns. But just as no entrepreneur can set *both* the price and the output of his product, no government can achieve *both* just outputs *and* just prices for factors of production in different regions.

As was noted above, the factor-price equalization theorem depends on a long list of heroic assumptions. Once these are modified to make even minimal concessions to realism and relevance, the theorem can at best proclaim a tendency to the equalization of factor-price ratios in different areas. In brief, any set of reasonably realistic assumptions about production conditions leads to the conclusion, confirmed by observation, that factor-price ratios differ between areas. The production assumption used in this book starts at this point. We assume that at least two factors of production are sufficiently immobile between areas to assure that ratios of factor supplies cannot be equalized between areas; and we assume that the rigorous conditions necessary for complete factor-price equalization with unequal factor-supply ratios (for example, zero transport costs and qualitatively identical natural resources in all areas) do not exist. In our analysis, therefore, at least one factor-price ratio must differ between areas. When the ratio of, say, the price of capital to the price of labour in one area differs from the same ratio in another area it may easily be proved that the "cost of production" of a commodity, for a given output, must in general differ between the two areas. (Consider a standard "isoquant" diagram with physical units of two factors of production measured along the two axes. Assume that the price ratio of these factors differs in the two areas. For a given total outlay, the family of total outlay lines for one area will then have a different slope than the total outlay lines for the other; in general, the two lines representing the same outlay in each area will intersect. Only by chance will such a pair of outlay lines both be tangent to any given isoquant; in general, production of the same output in each area will require a different total outlay in each area.)

In general, then, we may be sure that the per unit cost of producing automobiles in Windsor at any given output differs from the per unit cost of producing them in Detroit at the same output—though the per unit cost of producing at a *particular* output in Windsor may be the same as the per unit cost of producing at some *other* output in Detroit. Assertions that the costs of production "must" be the same in the two cities, presumably because of their geographical propinquity, reflect not common sense, but common error. Common sense requires us to recognize that the mere presence of the international border is a sufficient condition for factor-price ratios to differ between the two cities. Labour, we have assumed, is less than completely mobile across the international border; land and government, both important factors of production, are completely immobile across the border; and, although we assume complete capital mobility, the difference in interest rates in Canada and the United States indicates that in fact capital is less than completely mobile across the border. Since wages, interest, rent, and the price of government services all differ as between Detroit and Windsor, common sense alone would lead us to suspect what theory proves, namely, that for identical outputs the cost of producing automobiles, or any other commodity, will be different in the one city from that in the other.

It is indeed "difficult" to explain the locational pattern of most manufacturing output, either within a nation or between nations. But the "difficulty" is not conceptual; it is purely empirical. It derives in part from the complexity of actual production functions but mainly from the virtual absence of any public information about industries' actual costs. The question is what the intellectual response should be to a situation of complexity compounded by ignorance of the facts. All too often intellectual impatience leads governments, amateur economists, and even professional economists—especially those engaged in regional studies and in studies concerning the location of industry —to assume that, if we do not know the difference in production costs between two areas the difference must be zero, or at least insignificantly different from zero. This "conclusion" is presumably based on the circular reasoning that if there were a significant difference we would know about it. But it is surely unwise for governments to base policies on a "conclusion" that derives, by way of circular reasoning, from a combination of ignorance and impatience. Lack of knowledge about a complex situation should be treated as a challenge to provide the relevant knowledge, not as an excuse to pretend that it is not required.


## APPENDIX II

TRADE AND THE DIVISION OF LABOUR

A completely general theory of trade should surely apply not only to *all* geographic trade but also to interpersonal trade (the division of labour) and to trade between firms.

Let us use the simple "perfect mobility–perfect immobility" model; as we have seen, trade then implies the existence of at least two immobile factors in different proportions in different regions. Let us also, reasoning by analogy, identify immobile factors with inherited abilities in individuals (including abilities to learn certain things) and mobile factors with acquired abilities. It is a striking observation, as Adam Smith noted, that the propensity to trade is purely a *human* characteristic; all humans trade and no animal trades.[13] Our analogy suggests, then, that human individuals must be endowed with at least two inherited abilities in unequal proportions and that members of an animal species, by contrast, must either (*a*) be endowed with no inherited ability and all acquire (learn) the same abilities in the same proportions, or (*b*) be endowed with one inherited ability and learn all others in amounts that equalize their ability-ratios, or (*c*) be endowed with all abilities in the same proportions by inheritance— the "instinct" theory of animal behaviour.

The problem of inter-firm trade is very complex. Perhaps we should dispel it by viewing firms simply as groups of individuals and inter-firm trade as nothing but interpersonal trade. If, however, firms be viewed as "natural entities" that specialize in particular outputs and trade between themselves they must display some sort of comparative advantage. One suggestion follows from our "Rule of Two." In seeking to identify a firm economists have often fixed on one particular factor to explain its uniqueness—for example, entrepreneurship or capital-acquiring ability. If these assets are taken to be qualitatively different between firms, or if the "environment" in different firms differs, we have the "classical" view of comparative advantage; each firm is then assumed to have a unique production function. If such "immobile" factors are taken to be qualitatively identical between firms, we have the "modern" view of comparative advantage; the existence of comparative advantage would then require that each firm be endowed with at least *two* of these assets in proportions that differ from one firm to another.

---

[13]"Nobody ever saw a dog make a fair and deliberate exchange of one bone for another with another dog." *The Wealth of Nations* (Modern Library ed.), p. 13.

28

# 2

## The Cost of Protectionism
## with High International
## Mobility of Factors

Given the Ricardian assumption that factors of production, though completely mobile nationally, are completely immobile internationally, trade theory proves that real income per capita in a country with an effective[1] protective tariff will be lower than it would be in a free trade situation.[2] Does the proposition hold if we assume international mobility of the factors of production? Our first inclination is to say that it does, because (*a*) the excess costs above world costs of producing protected commodities must be paid for by the consumers of the commodities, and (*b*) the consumers must be the domestic population, since commodities produced at costs above world costs cannot be sold to foreign consumers. On the other hand, it seems paradoxical to talk of imposing costs on people who

[1] By effective protection we mean protection that results in protected production, i.e., production at costs above world costs. Whatever the intent of a tariff, it is not protective unless it actually protects something. If a tariff does not result in domestic production, or if domestic production takes no advantage of a tariff (i.e., if domestic costs in the "protected" industry are not above world costs) the tariff is ineffective. Industries which produce commodities that are subject to import duties, but which nevertheless export these commodities in significant volume, must by definition produce at costs no higher than world costs; the domestic tariffs on the commodities concerned are therefore ineffective. Tariffs that are ineffective according to the above definition may nevertheless have income-redistributing effects.
[2] A standard exception to this proposition can be derived by assuming that a country enjoys some degree of monopsony or monopoly power in the international market.

are internationally mobile, and who can therefore avoid the burden of a protective tariff in whole or in part by emigration to a country where the burden is either non-existent or lighter. If there is protected production there must be a burden; but since the costs of protection can be avoided by emigration there can be no burden. The apparent contradiction could, of course, be avoided by taking the position that it is impossible to create, or expand, protected industry by means of a tariff in a country whose population is not imprisoned within its own borders by the Ricardian assumption. The contention of this paper, however, is that a country *can* establish protected industry—manufacturing, let us say—within its borders even when its population is free to emigrate. Our problem is to show how this outcome is possible.

The problem may be rephrased by noting the converse of the proposition stated in our introductory sentence, namely, that a tariff must effect a reduction in real income per capita in a country in order to be effective, i.e., to lead to the development of protected production. Accordingly, if we can describe a mechanism by which a protective tariff results in a reduction of real income per capita in a country whose population is free to emigrate, we will have shown the tariff to be effective.

I

It must be noted immediately that, while the Ricardian assumption of complete international immobility of all factors is conceivable (however unrealistic), the opposite assumption of complete international mobility of all factors is not. One whole class of factors of production, namely, natural resources, including climate, soil, forests, mines, water power, and topography, is conceptually immobile; moreover, except in a few cases, it is impossible with present technology to produce these factors (or substitutes for them) at any reasonable cost. Geographical position, often an important factor of production in commercial activities, is also conceptually immobile. The polar opposite of the Ricardian assumption is therefore untenable. We might, of course, approach it as closely as possible by assuming complete mobility of all factors of production that are conceptually mobile. Given the world as it is, however, this would be a very unrealistic assumption, especially with respect to labour; it would also be an intellectually uninteresting one, because it would be equivalent to the assumption of a one-nation world, and would thus lead immediately to the conclusion that, ignoring transfer costs, the real income of all units of a homogeneous and mobile factor of production would be everywhere the same. Our model is therefore built on the assumption of high, but not complete, mobility of the inherently mobile factors. We assume complete international mobility of capital, but for labour we assume complete mobility along some international routes, and incomplete mobility along others.[3]

The argument of the paper is developed in terms of a three-area model composed of country $A$, country $B$, and a collectivity of all other countries, $C$. Like real countries, our countries occupy different positions in space so that movements of goods or factors between them involve transfer costs; they have endowments of natural resources that differ in size, composition, and quality; they have different climates; and they have different political and social institutions. These differences mean, on the one hand, that we are dealing with a world in which the factor-price equalization theorem is not applicable. On the other, they permit us to say that the comparative advantages of different countries in different lines of production depend on their natural resource endowments[4] and perhaps on such features of the human environment as governmental, legal, and social institutions. Because we assume less

[3]By mobility we mean, not movement, but the freedom to move. The existence of transfer costs hinders movement, but implies no reduction of mobility. Essentially, mobility means the legal freedom to move. By "incomplete mobility" we refer to a situation where there are legal restrictions on movement under certain specified conditions, and freedom to move under all other conditions. See also chap. 1, sec. II, above.

[4]We therefore contend that comparative advantage or disadvantage, in manufacturing as well as in primary production, depends on natural-resource endowment. Support for this contention may be found in my *Hydroelectricity and Industrial Development* (Cambridge, Mass., 1957), pp. 156–77.

31

than complete mobility of all mobile factors of production, and because movement involves transfer costs, there will, even in our world, be differences in the proportions of mobile factors in different countries, and these differences will also create comparative advantages; but comparative advantages that derive from this source will obviously be of less significance in our "high-mobility" model than in traditional models based on the assumption of international factor immobility. In fact we ignore this second source of comparative advantage, since the first seems quite capable of bearing by itself the burden of our "comparative advantage" assumptions. In our world therefore, comparative advantages are assumed to depend on the endowment of inherently immobile factors and to be invariant with respect to supplies of mobile factors. They are also assumed to be fixed during the period of time covered by the argument. (They are not, of course, fixed for ever; they will change as technology changes, since technology is an essential component of the very concept of natural resources, and perhaps also as human institutions change.)

The general assumptions underlying the argument are four in number: (1) no country has any monopoly or monopsony power in international markets; (2) full employment is continuously maintained in all countries; (3) no firm or industry produces under conditions of decreasing costs; and (4) all firms operate under competitive market conditions. Arguments from monopoly or oligopoly, even when industries are protected by tariffs, are eschewed.

The analysis proceeds by way of comparative statics. The comparison is between the economic situation in the protectionist country *B* before and after the adoption of protective tariffs. It should be noted that this "through-time" comparison is exactly equivalent to a "through-space" comparison of *B* with *A*, a free trade country, *provided that protectionism in* B *has no significant effect on economic magnitudes in* A.[5] The base for the latter comparison would be the relative position

[5]The reader may, if he wishes, think of *B* as a small country and of *A* as a large country. I shall not in this paper attempt to analyse the effects of protection in *B* on the economies of *A* and *C*; but I doubt that it is necessary to assume that *B*'s economy is small relative to *A*'s.

of $B$-magnitudes to $A$-magnitudes in the pre-protection situation; the influence of protection on $B$ would then be manifest in a changed relative position of $B$-magnitudes to $A$-magnitudes in the post-protection equilibrium. We shall make use of this "through-space" comparison at various points in the paper.

The model is based on the following specific assumptions:

(1) Country $A$ has no tariff. It has a comparative advantage in a few lines of non-manufacturing production, and a comparative advantage in a very wide range of manufacturing production. More specifically, it produces many non-manufactured goods economically at relatively small volumes to supply all or part of the domestic market, and a few such goods in large volumes to supply both domestic and export markets. By contrast, it produces most manufactured goods in large volumes for both domestic and export markets, while in a few manufacturing industries it produces economically only at small volumes to service all or part of the domestic market.[6]

(2) Country $B$ levies a tariff on all manufactured goods. Its comparative advantages are precisely the reverse of $A$'s; without a tariff its production pattern would therefore be precisely the reverse of $A$'s.

(3) The relative levels of per capita real income, $W$, in the three countries before protection in $B$ are as follows: $W_A = W_B > W_C$. If protection is effective $W_B$ will fall. We assume, nevertheless, that it will remain above $W_C$ by an amount greater than the costs of moving from $C$ to $B$. Accordingly, in the post-protection situation, our assumption is that $W_A > W_B > W_C$.

(4) Capital is completely mobile between all countries.

(5) No country restricts emigration.

[6]"Comparative advantage" must be thought of as a combination of two components, (1) potential cost advantage at zero output and (2) the change, if any, in cost advantage as output increases. The second component will be zero if the industry in question produces at constant costs. Under increasing costs comparative advantage will decline as output expands. Even with constant costs for each *industry*, the comparative disadvantage of a protected *sector* will increase as new industries, with larger and larger comparative disadvantages at zero output, are added to the sector.

33

(6) Labour is completely mobile between $A$ and $B$; $A$ does not restrict immigration from $B$, nor does $B$ restrict immigration from $A$.

(7) Country $B$ restricts immigration from $C$ according to the following rule: Immigration from $C$ is permitted whenever there is an excess demand for labour in the $B$ economy at the existing money wage, and is prohibited whenever the excess demand for labour is zero or negative. $A$ restricts immigration from $C$ according to a similar rule. Immigrants from $C$ are always available in unlimited quantity; the amount of immigration therefore depends entirely on the operation of the immigration rule. In effect, we assume that the supply of labour available to $A$ and $B$ is infinitely elastic, for increases in the supply, at the going money wage.[7]

Further assumptions will be introduced as the argument develops. Those already listed delineate the main boundaries of the argument. The model is intended to be realistic, and has been designed with an actual case in mind. Country $A$ is meant to be the United States; $B$, Canada; and $C$, Europe, or the rest of the world; the assumptions are intended to constitute a rough likeness (or at least a recognizable caricature) of the real-world situation of these three countries in, say, the second quarter of the twentieth century.[8]

[7]The analytical effect of this assumption, together with the assumption of full employment, is to freeze the money wage rate in $B$. The invariant money wage rate in $B$ is not a rigidity in the analysis; it simply serves as a standard against which to compare the movement of other variables. In particular, it does *not* fix the ratio of money wage in $B$ to the money wage elsewhere. If, for example, money wages in $B$ remain unchanged as labour productivity improves in all countries (including $B$), $B$'s money wage will fall in relation to money wages in other countries.

[8]It will be objected that the United States is not a free trade country. Our argument requires only the weaker assumption that the burden of protectionism in $A$ is lighter than the burden of protectionism in $B$, a proposition that will be more readily granted. Nevertheless, the large-scale export of a wide range of manufactured goods from the United States throughout the second quarter of the twentieth century implies a very low degree of effective protection to manufacturing industry in that country (see n. 1 above and chap. 4, sec. I) and leads me to believe that the stronger assumption is not wildly unrealistic.

It will also be objected that we overlook the severe restrictions on immigration to the United States inherent in the quota system adopted by that country in the early 1920's. However, native Canadian, and some native-born nationals of some countries, are not subject to immigration quotas. The quota system probably has a greater effect on the national composi-

34

One may find two "irrationalities" in the list of assumptions. *B*'s rule for restricting immigration from *C* suggests that *B* is unwilling to allow the real wage of its labour force to be reduced by unrestricted immigration from *C*. But as we shall see, protectionism in *B* involves both some immigration from *C* and a fall in real wages in *B*. Thus immigration from *C* and a fall in real wages are associated, though the association is not one of direct cause and effect since both result from the protectionist policy. Country *B* may be said, therefore, to allow immigration to reduce its real wage level, provided it does so through the medium of protectionism. The second "irrationality" is that *A* protects its labour force against unrestricted immigration from *C*, but not from *B*. What must be emphasized is that these "irrationalities" mirror the real-world situation and are not of our making. We seek to describe the real world, not to "improve" it by remaking it in the image of logical consistency.

The main purposes of the analysis are to show that protected production is possible under our assumptions, to determine the equilibrium size of the protected sector, and to show the effects of the protectionist policy on national income, factor supplies, and factor prices in *B*.

## II

In this section we assume that workers form a single, homogeneous factor of production—homogeneous, that is to say, with respect to productive services, not with respect to the concatenation of attitudes that we refer to as individual con-

---

tion of immigration to the United States than on its size. American restrictions do, however, reduce the mobility of many *naturalized* Canadians so far as emigration to the United States is concerned, and in this respect our model is at odds with the real world situation. Whether American immigration laws reduce emigration to the United States from Canada or whether the inability of some Canadians to emigrate increases the amount of emigration undertaken by native Canadians is not known.

The suggested "time period" has not been chosen at random. During the second quarter of the twentieth century, unlike the situation in more recent years, there was an almost unlimited supply of potential emigrants from Europe to North America, and the world superiority of American manufacturing was virtually unchallenged.

sumer preferences. For the moment we ignore capital, and conduct the argument solely in terms of labour. The existence of transfer costs of moving from one country to another means that $B$'s government can adopt, and make effective, a policy, such as protectionism, that results in a modest reduction in the real wage in $B$, without inducing large-scale emigration from the country. We define transfer costs to include the money costs of moving, the loss in psychic income, if any, involved in changing political allegiance, and the expected loss of income over the period "from job to job." Transfer benefits will be mainly the discounted value of additional income that is expected to result from the move. Net transfer costs will, by definition, be negative for emigrants and positive for non-emigrants at any given time. Since the calculations of both costs and benefits run largely in psychological terms (psychic income and expectations of future income being major considerations), individuals will probably differ widely in their assessments of the net benefits of emigration, even when the individuals concerned are similarly placed with respect to occupation, knowledge of opportunities abroad, and so on. What is important from the point of view of the economy as a whole is the level and elasticity of the supply of emigrants from $B$ as a function of the differential in real income per capita between $A$ and $B$. Whatever its absolute amount, emigration, which is induced indirectly by the growth of the protected sector through its effect in lowering the real wage in $B$ relative to $A$, will in turn tend to check the growth of the protected sector by reducing the market for its product.

This tendency, however, is opposed by simultaneous immigration from $C$ to $B$. Under the Ricardian assumption, the protected sector of an economy can expand only by attracting resources from other sectors of the same economy, at least one of which must therefore contract its output. Under our assumptions this result does not follow. Since immigration provides for unlimited supplies of labour at the existing wage rate, the protected sector can expand on the basis of immigrant labour at the existing money wage and thus need not draw labour from other parts of the domestic economy. How-

36

ever, since the tariff increases the prices of manufactured goods real wages must fall. As we have seen, the differential thus established between real wages in $A$ and $B$ leads to emigration from the non-protected sector; but since an unlimited supply of immigrant labour is available emigrants will be simultaneously replaced by immigrants at the same money wage. As a first approximation, then, we conclude that protectionism will not involve a reduction in output in the non-protected sector. At the same time, profit opportunities created by the tariff will result in an excess demand for labour in the protected sector; accordingly immigrants from $C$ will be allowed to enter the country until the excess demand is extinguished. Production thus grows in the protected sector and does not contract in the non-protected sector. We may tentatively conclude that protectionism increases $B$'s labour force and its national income, in both money and real terms, on the one hand, and on the other reduces the standard of living of $B$'s population.

This conclusion glosses over several difficulties that must now be discussed: the probable effect of protectionism on the price of capital in $B$; its probable effect on rent; and various repercussions of changes in factor price ratios.

A sharp distinction must be made between the price of capital goods and the price of capital (the rate of interest) in $B$. The former price will rise because we have assumed that $B$ levies a tariff on all manufactured goods, whether intermediate or final, producers' goods or consumers' goods. Thus if we compare a protected industry in $B$ with its unprotected equivalent in $A$ (equivalent in the sense that both industries face the same production function) it is clear that the $B$ industry will tend to use less machinery and more labour than the $A$ industry. (If technical coefficients are fixed, the higher cost of machinery in $B$ will have to be met entirely by the tariff protection, i.e., by the higher price of output in $B$.)

As to the interest rate in $B$, we suggest that it will probably be increased by the protectionist policy. Assuming for the moment that the capital supply in the non-protected sector of $B$'s economy remains unchanged as a result of protectionism, the capital required for the expansion of the protected sector will be met by imports from *A* or *C*. We assume that the capital imports into *B* are a small proportion of the total world supply of capital, so that the world interest rate will not increase. Nevertheless, there will be transfer costs of moving capital to *B*, so that while the capital is being imported *B*'s money rate of interest must rise in order to overcome these costs and attract imports. Will the rate remain above the world rate when equilibrium is re-established? An exchange risk is involved in any international investment, and the probable effect of protectionism in *B* will be to magnify this risk by setting in motion a chain of developments that will tend to reduce the world value of *B*'s currency.[9] Where imported capital is committed to a protected industry in *B* we must also remember that the output of that industry will be limited by the size of the domestic market. Investors in these industries thus forego the possibility of extraordinary gains that might accrue to them if they invested in an enterprise that could, if successful, command a large export market for its product. A wise capitalist investing in a protected industry will no doubt stipulate for a somewhat higher money return than would satisfy him if he were investing in an industry where money-making possibilities were greater. There is, finally, the probably insignificant risk that the tariff on the protected industry will be reduced at some time in the future. None of these arguments by itself seems strong enough to support a conclusion that the post-protection rate of interest in *B* must be appreciably above the pre-protection rate (or above the world rate). Nevertheless, the arguments all point in the same direc-

---

[9]If our provisional conclusions hold, namely, that protectionism will increase *B*'s population and national income, it is probable that *B*'s balance of trade will be adversely affected despite the growth of import-competing industries. Even though per capita imports of consumers goods fall, total imports of consumers goods may rise; similarly, if the import content of protected production is large the imports of intermediate goods may also rise. On the other hand, protection will do nothing to increase exports and will reduce them if domestic sales to the protected sector are substituted for export sales. Protectionism's influence on the balance of trade is therefore likely to tend to depreciate *B*'s currency. This tendency may be offset by protection-induced imports of capital during the period of expansion in the protected sector, but this effect will disappear when the equilibrium level of protected production is reached.

tion and, taken together, I think establish a probability that protection will tend to raise the rate of interest in $B$. Henceforth we brazenly suppose the probability to be a certainty. Accordingly, we conclude that protection raises the price of capital in $B$, and thus in $B$ relative to $A$. Again we reach the conclusion that coefficients of production in manufacturing will be more labour-intensive in $B$ than in $A$; protectionism will increase the money prices of both capital goods and of capital in $B$ relative to $A$, while under our assumptions money wages in $B$, and therefore in $B$ relative to $A$, will be unchanged.

Turn now to the non-protected sector of $B$'s economy. Here too, the effect of the change in factor prices resulting from protectionism will be to induce a substitution of labour for capital. Two questions arise: "Will production in the non-protected primary industries fall?" and "What happens to natural-resource rents?"[10] The prices of primary outputs will be unaffected by protectionism since we may assume that these prices are determined in world markets and are not appreciably affected by changes in $B$'s output.[11] With a rise in capital costs and unchanged money wages variable cost per unit of output in the primary sector will rise. Rents will therefore be reduced and the extensive margin of production will contract; the mobile factors thus released (labour or capital, or both) will emigrate or move to other sectors of the economy. However, the reduction of output will probably be small. Indeed it is realistic, I suggest, to think of all natural resource industries (except perhaps farming) earning rent in the pre-protection period; this situation could occur if *all* supplies of a natural resource were being exploited, or, more probably, if there were "gaps" in the "quality scale" of natural resources

[10]We identify the non-protected sector with the primary industry sector, and ignore the effect of protectionism on the other non-protected sectors of the economy, e.g., service industries, and non-protected manufacturing industries.

[11]We thus assume that the prices of primary industry inputs into the protected sector are unchanged by protectionism. Implicitly, we also assume that the protected sector and the primary sector do not compete for natural resources. This assumption is true by definition except in the case of land sites. Protectionism will undoubtedly tend to raise land rents in areas where the protected industries are located. See V. C. Fowke, *The National Policy and the Wheat Economy* (Toronto, 1957), pp. 67–8.

such that, although the highest-cost firm in the industry was intra-marginal, an additional firm would be submarginal. If rent *is* earned in all natural-resource industries in the pre-protection situation, protectionism will involve a reduction in rent without any reduction of output.

We now summarize, and in the process modify, our earlier provisional conclusions in the light of the above discussion of capital costs and rent. Since the net effect of protectionism on many economic magnitudes is a balance of positive and negative components, it will help us to gauge the sign of the net effect if we relate our summary to a particular situation. We consider a country (again with Canada in mind) whose comparative disadvantage in manufacturing over a fairly wide range of output and variety is quite small, so that a given "subsidy" (a given burden of protectionism per capita) will result in a considerable growth of output in the protected sector. To put the matter differently, we consider a situation where the supply curve of protected output is quite elastic with respect to small increases in the price of output.

Our first conclusion remains unchanged; the existence of costs of emigration permits of a reduction in per capita real income in $B$,[12] and thus makes it possible for a protective tariff to result in the growth of protected production.

Our second set of conclusions relates to the size of the protected sector and the effects of protection on factor supplies and national income in $B$. The reduction in real wages that accompanies the growth of the protected sector leads to emigration, and, under our assumptions, simultaneous immigration.[13] It is just barely conceivable that the tariff-induced

---

[12]The real income of resident capitalists will rise if the percentage increase in interest rates is greater than the percentage increase in the price level. But real wages will fall, and, given the normal weights of labour and capital in national income, real income per capita will almost certainly fall.

[13]The "displacement theory" of the relationship between immigration and emigration in Canada suggested that immigration led to the emigration of native Canadians. See Mabel F. Timlin, *Does Canada Need More People?* (Toronto, 1951), pp. 14–20, 76–82, for a statement of this theory, and for what I consider a successful ridiculing of it. We are suggesting that a "replacement mechanism" whereby emigrants are replaced by immigrants is at work in the Canadian economy; we do not suggest any replacement *theory* of either the motives of emigrants or immigrants or of the size of emigration and immigration. See *ibid.*, pp. 69–75.

40

emigration and immigration will be equal,[14] and that money national income will be unchanged. Such would be the case if, as a result of higher capital costs, there were a large reduction in output in the non-protected sector of $B$'s economy, and if the consequent reduction in the labour force and money national income originating in this sector exactly equalled the expansion of the labour force and money national income originating in the protected sector. Roughly speaking, the conclusions of our "high factor mobility" model would then correspond to the conclusions of the Ricardian model. Population size would be unchanged, though the population would be composed of different people, for the emigrants from the non-protected sector would not be the immigrants to the protected sector. Money national income would remain unchanged, but both real national income and real income per capita would fall. Something like the main classical conclusions thus emerge as a special case of our argument. But in my judgment the case is *very* special indeed.

When we apply the model to the "typical" case[15] of a country, such as Canada, where the excess costs of protected production are modest (the country's comparative disadvantage in the protected industries is slight), our preliminary conclusions seem the better part of the truth. Given only a small comparative disadvantage in manufacturing, there will be a large expansion in the protected sector before the associated rise in capital costs will result in any appreciable reduction of output in the non-protected sector. In this case we may be confident that net immigration and net capital inflow will both be positive; that national income in both money and real terms will increase, the latter by a smaller amount than the former; and that real income per capita will fall.

[14]Throughout much of Canada's history emigration and immigration have been of the same order of magnitude, and it was this observation that led to the "displacement theory." Our argument applies not to *total* immigration and emigration, but only to that part of both movements that is *induced by protectionism.*

[15]We consider the case typical because protective tariffs of reasonable levels in countries where manufacturing is subject to severe comparative disadvantages will probably not result in any significant amount of protected production, i.e., the tariffs will be largely ineffective. It is mainly those countries in which manufacturing is only moderately uneconomic that suffer significantly from protective tariffs on manufacturing.

But what determines the equilibrium size of the protected sector? To this question we can now give a formal, if uninformative, answer. The limiting factor may be either the size of the market available to the protected sector, or the amount of protection afforded it by the tariff. The less the comparative disadvantage of the sector, the less will be the effect of protectionism on the real wage, and thus on emigration, and the greater will be the effect on immigration, and, accordingly, the greater the growth of population, national income, and protected production. Nevertheless, comparative disadvantage increases with output (i.e., domestic costs rise relative to world costs as the quantity, or the variety, of protected production increases)[16] and the protected sector will expand only to the point where its marginal costs of output equal world prices plus the tariff. The tariff level in combination with rising costs thus sets one possible limit to protected production. This limit may be at a level of output that falls considerably short of satisfying domestic demand, in which case the excess domestic demand will be satisfied by imports that come in over the tariff. Alternatively, the protected sector will supply the entire domestic market when, at this level of output, marginal costs of protected production have not risen to the tariff level. In this case it will be the size of the home market that brings expansion to a halt. The market constraint will provide the solution in all cases where production takes place at constant costs (i.e., where comparative disadvantage does not increase as output expands), for there will then be no imports of the goods that are produced domestically. In no case, however, can protected production escape the home market since by definition the costs of such production exceed world costs. It is the domestic tariff, not foreign tariffs, that confines protected production to the home market.

Our third set of conclusions relates to production coefficients and income shares; these conclusions are held less confidently than the others since they derive from the rather inconclusive argument about the effects of protectionism on the rate of interest and on rent from natural resources. Protectionism, we

[16]See n. 6 above.

concluded, raises the price of capital relative to the price of labour in the country that adopts it. It follows that there will be a substitution of labour for capital in production functions throughout the economy. (There will be a substitution of labour for machinery in production functions because of the tariff-induced increase in the price of machinery, even if interest rates remain unchanged.) Higher capital costs will result in contraction of the non-protected sector, though we have suggested that this effect will be slight, and may be zero under realistic conditions, i.e., when all resources utilized in the pre-protection situation earn rent. Rent's share in the national income will decline relative to the shares of both labour and capital, both because income from natural resources will fall as a proportion of national income as the latter rises with the growth of the protected sector, and because rent per unit of natural resources will fall while money wages remain unchanged and the interest rate rises. What happens to the relative income shares of labour and capital will depend on the relative percentage changes in both the prices and quantities of these two factors.

### III

The preceding argument has been based on transfer costs; it is the existence of transfer costs which allows real wages to be reduced, and protectionism to become effective, even under our assumptions of high factor mobility. In this section we draw attention to a second mechanism by which a protectionist policy may reduce real income per capita in our model. The present argument in no sense duplicates or replaces the analysis of section II; it is, rather, an extension of that analysis, and has the effect of increasing the quantitative significance of several of the conclusions there developed.

The argument is based on the consideration that, over time, protectionism may lead to a significant change in the character of $B$'s population as a result of the immigration and emigration that is induced by the protective policy. Specifically, the

43

post-protection population—the original population less gross emigration plus gross immigration—may have a different attitude towards work and be prepared to offer the same labour services as the pre-protection population in return for a reduced real income; and it may be of a different average "quality," as measured, say, by average number of years of schooling per capita. Over a period of years, particularly if the protected sector in $B$ continuously expands, and thereby exerts a persistent downward pressure on real wages in $B$, a significant fraction of $B$'s pre-protection population may emigrate and be more than replaced by immigration.

This "population turnover" mechanism leads to some paradoxical conclusions. Protective tariffs, which in popular mythology are supposed to protect native labour from the competition of cheap foreign labour, may end up by bringing the cheap foreign labour to the protected country. In the process, of course, the immigrants' standard of living is raised. Protectionism in a rich country thus acts as a sort of international aid program, and becomes a means of transferring real income from the non-emigrants in the rich country to immigrants from the poor country. (This is not to say that protectionists should be allowed to parade as philanthropists; there are far more effective ways of granting aid to low-income foreigners than by protecting domestic industry—a relaxing of immigration restrictions, or tariffs, for example.)

For analytical purposes we need only note that the "population turnover" may in itself lead to a significant reduction in real wages per person in $B$; it thus underwrites the "transfer costs" argument of section II. Real wages per person in $B$ will be reduced as the population "turns over" if ($a$) the new population displays a lower marginal disutility for work than did the former population, or if ($b$) the average quality of the new population in terms of skill and years of schooling is lower than that of the former population. The first factor lowers real wages per efficiency unit and will improve the productivity of $B$'s economy, while the second factor may leave real wages per efficiency unit unchanged and will reduce

44

productivity. In both cases, however, real wages per person will be reduced. If the average quality of the new population is higher than that of the old, we reach the anomalous conclusion that the quality and productivity of $B$'s population will increase while real wages per person are being reduced.

The practical significance of the "population turnover" argument is unknown since we lack empirical data even to determine which of the various possible outcomes mentioned is likely to be operative, much less the data needed to assess its quantitative significance. It is clear that under our assumptions protectionism is likely to change the composition of a country's population, and in the process to lower real wages per person; what is far from clear is whether the quality of the population, however measured, is likely to be raised or reduced by the turnover.

## IV

Our analysis casts indirect light on some probable "long-run" or "dynamic" effects of a protectionist policy that is continued over a long period of time. Of what does "the burden of protectionism" consist?

From the point of view of $B$'s pre-protection population, the conclusions of our analysis parallel the conclusions of the dismal science about the effects of protectionism on a country's standard of living. We have not, however, proved that the adverse effect of protectionism on a country's standard of living will be as great under our assumptions of high factor mobility as it would be under the Ricardian assumption. Indeed, the possibility of escape by emigration from the burden of protectionism will surely mean that the burden will be less than when the same degree of protectionism is imposed on a captive population. But even if the "burden of protectionism" is lighter with international factor mobility than with international factor immobility, we have no clear idea of its dimensions under either assumption.

45

Conventional measures of the burden[17] tell us how much the real income of a post-protection population could be increased by imagining that it could buy its domestically produced protected output at world prices, all other things remaining unchanged. But we have seen that under our assumptions other things are far from being unchanged by a protectionist policy —and our assumptions are not so specialized that they apply only to the three actual countries that are the prototypes of A, B, and C. Effective tariffs, as we have seen, affect both the levels and proportional relationships of factor supplies, factor prices, and income shares in the protectionist country. Coefficients of production are affected throughout the economy, and of course the industrial pattern of output is altered. If the "free-trade" situation in B with respect to factor supplies and factor prices represented a "Paretian optimum" adjustment of mobile factors to the inherent geographical potentiality of the country, the post-protection situation certainly does not. The economic inefficiency implicit in this deviation from a Paretian optimum is part of the true burden of protectionism. A "cash cost" measure of the burden of protectionism made under the assumption that factor supplies and factor prices are invariant with respect to commercial policy ignores this part of protectionism's burden on the standard of living, and as a measure

[17]See H. G. Johnson, "The Cost of Protection and the Scientific Tariff," *Journal of Political Economy*, August, 1960, pp. 327–45; J. H. Young, *Canadian Commercial Policy*, (Ottawa, 1957), chap. 7. In passing it may be noted that Young's refutation (pp. 89–93) of arguments to the effect that protectionism has increased Canada's population does not touch our argument. Young always supposes that a fall in real wages in B will result in an increase in emigration and a decrease in immigration; our model supposes that *both* emigration and immigration will be increased, the latter by a greater amount than the former. It should also be noted that Young's *total* cost of protection is the difference between national income with a tariff and the supposed national income without a tariff, factor supplies and money incomes remaining unchanged. If we define the *total* burden as the difference between pre-protection and post-protection national income, the *total* cost of protectionism in our model is negative. Since protectionism in our model raises the real wages of immigrants by comparison with their real wages in their country of origin, the only unambiguous meaning that can be attached to "the cost of protection" is the reduction in the per capita real income of the non-immigrant portion of B's post-protection population. We argue in the text that the per capita cost of protectionism implicit in Young's calculation is likely seriously to underestimate the burden of protectionism so defined.

of the total per capita burden is therefore subject to an indeterminate downward bias.

In addition a true reckoning of the long-run costs of protectionism would have to take into account its possible effects on the quality of the country's economic life. We have noted the possibility that the quality of the country's labour force may be adversely affected; in particular, unregulated emigration may be more highly selective with respect to quality than administered immigration. Protectionism also tends to be subversive of the quality of a country's non-human productive apparatus. We have shown reason to think that the rate of interest will rise relative to wages in a protectionist country. Salter has shown[18] how this tendency will defer "the date of obsolescence" and result in a larger proportion of an industry's capital equipment being relatively old and outmoded. Furthermore, the higher ratio of capital to labour costs in a protectionist country as compared with a free trade country will mean that the "best-practice plant" in the former country will use less capital-intensive techniques than the best-practice plant in the same industry in the latter country. To the extent that "high productivity" is associated with highly capital-intensive techniques, the protectionist country will therefore always be a "step behind" the free trade country in production practices.[19]

One final and rather wild broadside may be directed in the general direction of the protectionist camp. From the data of economic history we may hazard the guess that a disproportionate number of large fortunes in any country derive directly or indirectly from industries in which the country enjoys a large comparative advantage. A protectionist policy which increases a country's population by promoting the growth of industries that suffer a comparative disadvantage may thus be a potent factor working against, not the number of large fortunes, but the number of large fortunes per million population in a protected economy. If this be so, such things as research

[18]W. E. G. Salter, *Productivity and Technical Change* (Cambridge, 1960).
[19]See H. C. Eastman, "The Canadian Tariff and the Efficiency of the Canadian Tariff," *American Economic Review*, May, 1964, pp. 437–48.

funds and university endowments may be rather few and far between in protectionist countries. More generally, the conclusion that a policy whose effect on the standard of living of a country is necessarily adverse must necessarily reduce domestic capital formation per capita over the long run seems incontrovertible. Our conclusion that protective tariffs are likely to increase the capital supply of a country thus implies that the share of the domestically created component of a country's total capital supply must fall when the country moves from free trade to protectionism.

Much more important, perhaps, than the short-run reduction in a country's standard of living as a result of protectionism are the long-run tendencies of a protective tariff policy to reduce the per capita income-creating, and therefore the per capita capital-creating, capabilities of the economy. Such a result is, after all, inherent in any policy which subsidizes industries that are inefficient by world standards at the expense of industries that are efficient by world standards. Under our assumptions, though not under Ricardo's, a protected economy will grow in terms of population and national income. But growth in these total magnitudes is nevertheless accompanied by decline in the standard of living; economic growth in a protected economy thus tends to be bought at the expense of the *quality* of economic life, including, in extreme cases, the quality of the country's population. A rich country can easily afford the reduction of its standard of living that is the short-run consequence of protectionism; how a continuous depression of its standard of living over time reacts on its income-generating and wealth-accumulating capabilities is quite another question, and one that is but dimly understood. But Ricardo's intuition about the importance of the law of comparative advantage for the wealth of nations seems to remain valid, and perhaps even to gain in significance, when his restricting assumption about the international immobility of the factors of production is relaxed.

48

# 3

## On the High Cost of Maintaining a Tariff

There is no hard and fast relationship between a tariff rate and a rate of protection; a uniform *ad valorem* tariff of, say, 20 per cent may in fact give any rate of protection from zero to infinity to different industries at the same time or to the same industry at different times. So commonplace is this proposition that familiarity seems to have bred contempt, with the result that analysis of the economic significance of the difference between tariff rates and protection rates has been slighted. International trade theorists, when analysing protection, have normally assumed a one-to-one relationship between the two rates purely as a matter of analytical convenience. Economic historians, when writing on the effects of tariffs, have normally made the same assumption, despite the fact that in the context of historical work, where changing economic trends are likely to result in changes in the rate of protection implied by a given tariff rate, the assumption is surely indefensible.

The lack of any clear understanding of how a tariff structure affects an economy over time provides a good illustration of the great communication barrier that continues to separate economic theory and economic history. Trade theorists, in their studies of tariffs, concern themselves almost exclusively with the economic effects of the *imposition* of a tariff (or, what is the same thing, an increase in an existing tariff) and thus deal explicitly only with the reactions of an economy to a once-for-all disturbance. This analysis is directly useful to

49

the historian in understanding economic trends only during the transition period, presumably limited to three or four years, while an economy is adjusting to a newly legislated tariff schedule. What happens thereafter? Comparative statics does not ask this question, but if one insists on inferring an answer to it from existing theory that answer would surely be "nothing"; the effects of a tariff, theory seems to imply, are exhausted in a once-for-all change in the *levels* of economic variables, and have no relevance to future *trends* in those variables.[1] Economic historians seem not to have accepted this inference, for many of them write as if they believed that a tariff provides for continued growth in the economy. So far as I know there is not the slightest theoretical justification for this view in the existing literature, apart from a general appeal to the infant industry argument.[2] In this paper I shall argue that a constant tariff is indeed likely to lead to continuing growth *in the protected sector*, but of course if the protected sector grows relative to the rest of the economy the effect will be to *reduce* the national growth rate, measured in terms of per capita national income.

# I

To show how an economy with a constant tariff will react to continuous changes in protection over time, it would be useful to have a few formal definitions. Let $t$ be an *ad valorem* tariff

[1] E. F. Denison, *The Sources of Economic Growth in the United States* (Supplementary Paper no. 13 published by the Committee for Economic Development, Washington, 1962), emphasizes that the removal of tariffs, and most other policies that remove obstacles to the efficient allocation of resources, "are one-time actions . . .; once taken, they cannot be repeated." (p. 275) It is also true, however, that the maintenance of a constant tariff involves recurrent decisions not to dismantle it, and that the continuation of a free trade policy involves recurrent decisions not to levy tariffs.

[2] In an incautious moment H. G. Johnson allowed himself to write ". . . if protectionists happen to be correct in their claim that protection increases an economy's rate of growth. . . ." ("The Cost of Protection and the Scientific Tariff," in the *Journal of Political Economy*, August, 1960, p. 339) But the *imposition* of protection certainly *reduces* the growth rate; and in the present essay it is shown that the *continuance* of protection will in all probability also reduce growth rates.

levied on the importation of all manufactured goods. Define the *rate of protection*, represented by $c$, as the percentage by which a weighted average of the per unit costs of production of protected goods that are produced domestically exceeds an identically weighted average of the duty-free import prices of the same goods.[3] Let the volume of protected output, measured in physical (i.e., constant dollar) units, be $x$. I then define the *amount* of protection, $P$, as the *total* excess cost of protected production,[4] so that $P = cx$. By the *burden* of protection I shall mean the amount of protection per member of the labour force, or $P/L (= cx/L)$.

The purpose of the analysis is to show how $P$ and $P/L$ change over time in an economy with a constant tariff. Both components of the amount of protection, $c$ and $x$, are subject to change through time. The volume of protected output, $x$, depends on both demand and supply conditions in the protected sector. As to the former, it should be noted that a change in the demand for protected output must originate in the domestic economy since foreign demand is zero; protected output is produced at costs in excess of world costs and therefore cannot, in the absence of export subsidies or dumping arrangements, be exported. Supply conditions are represented in part by $c$, which is a measure of the cost disadvantage of protected production. The rate of protection, $c$, will vary as domestic factor prices change in relation to foreign factor prices, but until the last section of the paper I ignore this source of variation. Throughout the main argument, variation in $c$ is assumed to result only from changes in the "technological" differential between home and foreign production, i.e., from changes in domestic factor productivities relative to foreign factor productivities.[5] I do not analyse cases where

[3]If, alternatively, the rate of protection were defined so as to increase as the ratio of domestic output to competitive imports increased, the rate would go to infinity when a tariff resulted in the elimination of imports.
[4]The argument ignores the consumption cost of a tariff; see Johnson, "The Cost of Protection and the Scientific Tariff," for a lucid analysis of both the production and consumption costs of a tariff under static assumptions.
[5]I assume that technology in the sense of *knowledge* of possible production techniques is always world-wide, i.e., that the transport costs of knowledge are zero, and that no country can have an advantage in knowledge over

costs in protected industries change relative to costs in other domestic industries; such changes at home are assumed to be matched by the same changes abroad, so that the competitive relationship between protected production and imports will be unaltered. It should be stressed that the output of protected industries can be changed by an alteration in supply conditions only when these change *in relation to* supply conditions abroad, for only in this way can a change take place in the cost of producing protected products relative to the cost of importing the same products.

Thus the effect over time of technological changes and shifts in demand is almost certain to produce changes in both the *amount* of protection ($P$) and the *burden* of protection ($P/L$) in a protected economy even when the tariff is kept constant. The problem is to show how $P$ and $P/L$ are likely to change over time, how this change will affect the economy, and in particular how it will affect growth rates of national income and national income per capita.


## II


The ground rules of this game are set out in the following five subsections.

(1) The argument makes use of two models, a "standard" model in which all factor supplies are assumed to be fixed, and a "variant" model in which some factor supplies change as factor requirements in the protected sector change. In both the standard and variant models a three-factor production function (land, labour, and capital) is assumed. In the variant model land is assumed to be completely immobile; its supply is therefore fixed. Capital is assumed to be perfectly mobile at the existing pattern of national interest rates, and "the" rate of interest is assumed to be set in a world market; in the domestic economy, therefore, capital supplies are always

---

another country. Countries differ, however, in their factor supplies, and especially in their natural resource endowments; the same technological change applied to different factor-supply situations will therefore produce differential productivity improvements as between countries.

adjusted to capital requirements at the going interest rate by imports or exports of capital. Labour is assumed to be mobile, but only in a specified sense. Migration is assumed to be a function, not of international differences in per capita income, but of international differences in the volume of "job opportunities"—expressed as international differences in the excess demand for labour at the existing money wage rate. An increase in the volume of protected output creates an excess demand for labour, and results in immigration; since nothing in the model creates an excess demand for labour in those countries to which domestic labour might emigrate (i.e., those countries where real wages are higher than in the domestic economy) no emigration will occur; accordingly the gross immigration resulting from the increase in protection is also net immigration.[6]

Three characteristics of the variant model should be noted. First, changes in protected output are effected by changes in the domestic supplies of labour and capital rather than, as in the standard model, by transfers of resources between the protected and unprotected sectors. Second, the assumed differences in the mobility of labour and capital imply differences in the behaviour of the prices of these factors. Perfect mobility of capital implies that the *ratio* of the domestic interest rate to the foreign interest rate remains constant, while the level of the domestic rate varies with the world rate. The assumption about labour mobility implies that the *level* of money wages in the domestic economy is fixed, so that the ratio of domestic to foreign wages will vary as the foreign wage rate varies. Third, the assumption of fixed factor supplies in the standard model means that a change in GNP will necessarily be accompanied by a change in GNP per capita in the same

---

[6]This type of model is described more fully in the previous essay. In that essay, however, the assumed migration function was slightly different. As in the present essay, gross immigration was assumed to depend solely on the appearance of an excess demand for labour in the domestic economy. Gross emigration, however, was previously made to depend on a reduction in domestic income per capita relative to income per capita abroad; in the present essay it is made to depend solely on the development of an excess supply of labour in the domestic economy. In the present model international differences in per capita income determine the *direction* but not the *volume* of migration flows.

direction and by the same percentage; in the variant model, however, these two magnitudes may move by different percentages and in different directions because of changes in the size of the labour force (population).

(2) The analysis is divided into two sections: a "constant costs" case, where the excess cost of protected production is assumed to be the same at all outputs; and an "increasing costs" case, where the excess cost per unit of protected output is assumed to increase as the size of the sector expands.

(3) In the standard model changes in the amount of protection ($P$) and the burden of protection ($P/L$) are said to produce changes in GNP and GNP per capita growth rates in the *opposite* direction. Conclusions from any "comparative statics" analysis can of course be expressed in terms of growth rates, simply by defining a time period as the time required to move from one equilibrium to the other; in the present case, for example, the growth rate in the burden of protection resulting from, say, a shift in demand for protected output, is the difference in the burden between the two equilibria expressed as a percentage of the burden at the first equilibrium. The proposition, then, is that in the standard model a positive growth rate of the amount (and therefore the burden) of protection, other things equal, amounts to a reduction in the GNP and GNP per capita growth rates in the economy by comparison with what they would otherwise have been.[7]

In the variant model the same proposition applies to the burden of protection and the per capita rate, but not to the amount of protection and the GNP rate. GNP may increase as the result of an increase in factor supplies; and even if the amount of protection increases, GNP may increase more. Thus in the variant model a constant tariff may increase *both* the amount of protection *and* the GNP; if the former grows at a slower rate than the latter the constant tariff will increase

[7]This direct translation of changes in the amount of protection into changes in aggregate growth rates implicitly denies that any economic significance should be attached to the statistical "shift effects" that affect measured GNP and GNP per capita when resources are transferred between sectors with different measured "productivities." On this matter see the appendix to this chapter.

the GNP growth rate by comparison with what it would otherwise have been.

But what, explicitly, *is* the comparison we make? What would the growth rates "otherwise have been?" To visualize the comparison imagine that, at a given point in time institutional arrangements are made in the economy under study that will (*a*) prevent *P* from ever increasing beyond its present level, and (*b*) if, at some future date, *P* falls, prevent it from ever increasing beyond its new, lower level. It is with this hypothetical situation, which I shall from now on refer to as the "control situation," that the constant tariff economy is compared.[8] To fulfil the conditions specified for the control situation by tariff policy alone (if that were possible) would require an *inconstant* tariff, i.e., one that was continually changed to prevent *P* from increasing as supply and demand conditions in the protected sector changed. In brief, I compare growth rates in the constant tariff economy with the growth rates that would be established in an economy where the same tariff *has operated* in the past but will not be allowed *to operate* in the future, except in so far as existing enterprises that depend on protection are concerned. The comparison is not between protection and free trade, but between the perpetuation of an old tariff in full vigour and a situation where old vested interests are protected but no new vested interests will be tolerated; such a comparison allows us to identify the costs of *continuing* a tariff.

(4) It is important that the reader keep the nature of our

[8]The "control situation" may be visualized as the situation that would exist if the state were (*a*) to transform all existing protection into a set of conditional subsidies, (*b*) to remove all tariffs, and (*c*) to increase general taxation sufficiently to compensate for the loss of customs receipts and provide for the new subsidies. Currently protected firms that registered themselves as such would receive annual subsidies to the extent of their losses *on the present scale of production* for a period of, say, twenty years. The present cost of protection would continue to be borne, but removal of the tariff would prevent it from affecting future trends in the economy and increasing the future cost of protection. The scheme amounts to a sort of "pensioning off" of present vested interests and has obvious similarities with arrangements actually made to pension off workers rendered surplus by rapid technological change. Governments inhibited from dismantling a tariff structure by fear of the short-run consequences of such a move might consider the scheme, for under it no employer and no employee would have to change his present employment as a result of tariff removal.

comparison in mind in order to interpret our conclusions correctly. For example, if it is found that in a constant tariff economy a particular development "increases the burden of the tariff" (and therefore reduces the GNP per capita growth rate) the increase *is relative to what the burden would have been in the control situation*; the actual burden of the tariff may increase, decrease, or remain unchanged. The question is whether any normative significance may be attached to our conclusions. Let us see.

Suppose that the Canadian tariff involved a reduction of the average consumer's income by 5 per cent in 1880 and that since then, during which time income per capita has, say, quadrupled, the burden has never exceeded 5 per cent. Are we then to say that the burden has not increased over time? (The burden in dollars will have quadrupled, but let us agree to ignore the possibility that the burden should be defined in absolute terms and continue to regard it as a percentage concept.) To do so is to interpret the intent of the original legislation in a particular way. Implicitly, it is argued that in 1880 the Canadian people agreed to reduce their income by up to 5 per cent in perpetuity in order that the manufacturing sector of their economy would, at any given time in the future, be larger than it would have been without the tariff. This position is certainly tenable, and if it is held our conclusions are misleading, for if the burden of the tariff had remained at 5 per cent of actual per capita income over time the conclusion of the present analysis, based on the comparison described above, would be that the burden had increased (and that the growth rate of GNP per capita had been reduced).

Though tenable, the position outlined above concerning the intent of the original tariff is far from mandatory. It would be easier, I think, to provide documentary support for another position, namely, that the original tariff was proposed and accepted on the basis of some vague version of the infant industry argument. In this case the tariff would be thought of as a species of economic pump-priming, a once-for-all operation to boost the economy into self-sustained growth. The implication is that in the normal course of events the tariff burden would decline through time, and that if it failed

56

to do so the burden as time went on would in fact be greater than had been anticipated. Our comparison is meant to reflect one version of this position. It is not based on a "term tariff" concept under which all tariffs would be removed after a definite length of time, though this concept would be consistent with a strict infant industry position. It is based on a rather weaker version of the infant industry view, namely, on the supposition that at some time after the original imposition of the tariff continuing subsidies that were the equivalent of the tariff protection then being utilized would be substituted for tariffs, and that no new future output would be protected either by subsidies or tariffs. Our position, then, is that if over time the burden of the tariff fails to fall by as much as it would have fallen under these institutional arrangements, the policy must be judged a failure. That is the normative significance to be attached to conclusions such as "the burden has increased" even if the actual burden measured as a percentage of per capita income has remained unchanged, or has fallen slightly. To put the matter another way, our conclusions may be interpreted as a measure of the failure of infant industry hopes to be realized.[9]

(5) Throughout the analysis I assume that all industries, including protected industries, produce under conditions of perfect competition, i.e., that price always equals marginal cost (including normal profits). The argument runs from one point of long-run equilibrium to another such point; no use is made of short-run equilibria based on abnormal profits, unemployment, or overemployment. The main argument, in section IV, is based on partial equilibrium analysis; in particular, the effect of changes in protected output on the balance of payments is ignored. A brief discussion of some features of the general equilibrium implied by the partial analysis is given in section IV.

The analysis in section III deals explicitly only with cases

[9]Two interesting papers by H. G. Johnson discuss in detail the tariff structures appropriate to different motives for protectionism: "Tariffs and Economic Development: Some Theoretical Issues," *Journal of Developmental Studies*, October, 1964, pp. 3–30; "An Economic Theory of Protectionism, Tariff Bargaining, and the Formation of Customs Unions," *Journal of Political Economy*, June, 1965, pp. 256–83.

of increases in demand and decreases in costs; these are the primary conditions for growth, and growth seems to be considered the normal economic condition. The analysis is symmetrical, of course, and the negatives of the conclusions arrived at will apply to cases of decreases in demand and increases in costs.

## III

### 1. CONSTANT COSTS

In Diagram 3.1, *SS* represents the domestic supply curve of protected production. It must be interpreted as a weighted average of the individual supply curves of all protected industries (which produce at anywhere from 100 to 120 per cent of world costs) the weights being the values of production of each product; the *x* axis is therefore calibrated in units of "dollars' worth of output at world prices." The line *WW* is a similarly weighted supply curve of imports of the same products and represents the world price of protected domestic output. The line *TT* is the supply price of imports to domestic

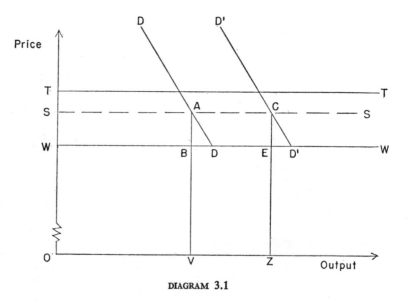

DIAGRAM 3.1

58

consumers, i.e., $WW$ plus a uniform *ad valorem* tariff of, say, 20 per cent. The line $DD$ is the demand curve for protected output of a "representative consumer," representative specifically in the sense of having an average income and a typical pattern of tastes. The area $SWBA$ is what we have previously referred to as the burden of protection ($P/L$); the amount of protection ($P$) is this area times the labour force.

*(a) Increase in Demand.* Consider a shift in the demand curve to $D^1D^1$ (which we also interpret as a shift over the time interval from time $D$ to time $D^1$). We must proceed on the "equiproportional" assumption that the shift leaves the pattern of demand for different protected products unchanged, since otherwise the weights used to construct $SS$ would change and the $SS$ curve would itself shift as a result of the shift in demand. (The $SS$ curve will probably be insensitive to small changes in most weights, so that in practice the assumption need not be quite so restrictive.) With a constant tariff the burden of protection will increase by $ABEC$, i.e., from $SABW$ to $SCEW$. (If the increase in demand results from a change in tastes, with income unchanged, the individual's burden of protection increases relative to his income; if the shift results from increased income, with unchanged tastes, and if we make the reasonable assumption that his income elasticity of demand for manufactured goods is greater than one, his burden of protection will still increase as a percentage of his income. But even when the income elasticity is low, so long as it is greater than zero, an increase in income will shift the $DD$ curve to the right and the burden of protection will increase in absolute terms.) An increase in demand therefore increases both the burden and the amount of protection in a constant tariff economy. In the control situation the increased demand of $VZ$ per person would have been satisfied by imports at a cost of $BVZE$, rather than by domestic production at the higher cost of $AVZC$; the increase in real income would therefore have been larger by $ABEC$. Thus a constant tariff reduces both the GNP and GNP per capita growth rates in an economy whenever there is an increase in demand for protected output.

59

In the variant model, the same increase in demand *increases* GNP (at world prices) by *BVZE* times the population, since this amount of production is added by the immigration of factors, rather than, as in the standard model, being transferred from the unprotected to the protected sector. The GNP growth rate will therefore *increase* as a result of the constant tariff; in the control situation the increased demand would have been served entirely by imports and domestic GNP would have remained unchanged. So far as GNP per capita is concerned, however, the conclusions drawn from the standard model apply unchanged in the variant model, provided only that the immigrants in the latter model have the same tastes and incomes as the "original" inhabitants; the burden of protection is increased by *ABEC* and the GNP per capita rate is accordingly reduced. The constant tariff in the variant model therefore results in a divergence between the GNP and GNP per capita growth rates when demand increases; indeed the rates move in opposite directions.

*(b) Decrease in Costs.* Consider now an equiproportional fall in the cost curves of protected industries; the fall is assumed to result from a domestic productivity increase in protected industries relative to productivity experience in the same industries abroad. (An uneven reduction in costs would alter patterns of consumption and thus change the position of the demand curve; again, however, shifts in the demand curve will probably be quite insensitive to small variations in cost reductions among protected industries.)

Rather surprisingly, no firm inference can be made about the probable shift, if any, in the *SS* curve as a result of the postulated fall in costs. Suppose a five percentage point fall in domestic costs in protected industries relative to world costs in the same industries abroad. Domestic industries that formerly produced at 100 to 105 per cent of world costs will now be on a free trade basis, and the burden of protection on the domestic economy, and domestic consumers, will thereby be reduced. But, by the same token, industries that formerly did not exist in the domestic economy because their potential costs were 120 to 125 per cent of world costs, will now enter the economy and produce at 115 to 120 per cent of world costs. We know nothing about the *volume* of formerly protected output that disappears into the unprotected area relative to the *volume* of newly protected output that now appears. In such cases of complete ignorance the standard ploy is to assume that one unknown magnitude equals the other. On this assumption the fall in domestic costs will leave the *SS* curve precisely where it was before the fall occurred. By the same appeal to ignorance we may suppose that the *DD* curve, which now applies to a new "basket" of protected products, remains unchanged.

On these assumptions, both GNP and GNP per capita in the standard model will remain unchanged despite the favourable cost experience, since the reduction in both the burden and the amount of protection resulting from the exit of some protected industries will be exactly matched by the increased burden and amount of protection resulting from the arrival of new industries, each demanding its toll. In the control situation, both GNP and GNP per capita would have increased since the favourable cost change would have removed existing industries from the protected rolls, and the increase would not have been offset by the setting up of newly protected industries. Thus with a cost decrease, as with an increase in demand, a constant tariff will reduce both growth rates in the standard model relative to the growth rates in the control situation. What has happened is that the constant tariff has translated all the benefits that should have resulted from the differentially favourable cost experience in previously protected industries into the excess costs of newly protected industries.

In the variant model, the identical analysis again applies to the individual consumer and to the GNP per capita rate. The analysis of GNP is, however, more complex.

Consider, first, what happens in the control situation. The differentially improved productivity (which we may consider to apply to *all* manufacturing, protected and unprotected alike) will have reduced labour requirements in manufacturing, and will thus have tended to lead to net emigration.

61

On the other hand, the reduction in manufacturing costs will have led to the expansion of some old industries by putting them on an export basis, will have brought some new industries into the control economy, and will thus have tended to produce net immigration. The increase in income per capita resulting from the productivity gain will also have produced an increase in GNP. On balance it is impossible to say which way GNP will move in the control situation.

All these things will also happen in the constant tariff economy under the conditions of the variant model. But GNP in the constant tariff economy will be subject to an additional positive component as the constant tariff brings newly protected industries, and thus new factor supplies, into the economy. The effect of the *tariff*, therefore, as distinct from the effects of the cost reduction, is to increase GNP in the variant model relative to the control situation. A decrease in costs in the variant model therefore has at least one effect in common with that of an increase in demand; the constant tariff creates a divergence between GNP and GNP per capita growth rates, increasing the former and depressing the latter.

If our "assumption from ignorance" be rejected, and both the *SS* and *DD* curves in Diagram 3.1 be allowed to shift as the result of the differential decrease in costs, the burden of protection may be either increased or decreased. If it is increased the conclusions already stated about the GNP per capita rate apply *a fortiori*. If it is decreased, the decreases resulting from some combination of the downward shift of costs in existing protected production and a shift to the left of the *DD* curve must have more than offset the increase resulting from the advent of newly protected industries. In the control situation the same decreases would not have been offset by any positive component of new protection; accordingly, in the constant tariff economy the decrease in the burden will be smaller, and the GNP per capita growth rate therefore lower, than in the control situation. A parallel argument applies to the amount of protection and the GNP rate. Even if GNP falls in the control situation, it will fall less in the constant tariff economy as the result of the addition of newly protected industries; accordingly the GNP rate in the constant tariff economy will rise relative to the GNP rate in the control situation. Again there will be divergence between the two rates in the constant tariff economy. The "assumptions from ignorance" are therefore seen to have been a matter of convenience rather than of substance; when they are dropped no conclusion is altered.

In summary, the "constant costs" analysis leads to the following two conclusions. (1) A constant tariff, in the standard model, reduces both GNP and GNP per capita growth rates in an economy whenever demand for protected output increases and whenever the cost of production in protected industries falls relative to costs in the same industries abroad. (2) In the variant model, a constant tariff has the same effect on the GNP per capita growth rate, but acts to increase the GNP rate; accordingly a constant tariff will produce divergence between these two growth rates in an economy that displays the characteristics of the variant model.

(Let me state, just this once, the negatives of the conclusions. In the unlikely event that the size of the protected sector in a constant tariff economy decreases, through some combination of a decrease in demand for protected goods and an increase in the relative cost of protected production, actual growth rates in the standard model will be identical with those in the control situation; in both cases the amount of protection will fall and the burden of protection will be lightened. Growth rates in the variant model will also be identical with those in the corresponding control situation. GNP will fall since net emigration will result from the contraction of the protected sector, while GNP per capita will rise, as the burden of protection is lightened; a constant tariff will therefore lead to convergence between the two actual rates, with the per capita rate rising and the total rate falling.)

## 2. INCREASING COSTS

Unlike Diagram 3.1, which referred only to protected manufacturing, Diagram 3.2 relates to all manufacturing, both protected and unprotected. It depicts a situation in which

63

domestic costs of production rise in relation to world costs as domestic output increases. Domestic output is assumed to be such a small proportion of world output that world costs are unaffected by changes in home production. The $x$ axis is again calibrated in "dollars' worth of output at world prices." The demand curves, which in Diagram 3.1 were weighted averages of demand curves for protected output, are now the representative consumer's true demand curves for all manufactured goods—both protected and unprotected domestic production and imports. The supply curves are now true aggregated supply curves, constructed by summing horizontally the domestic supply curves for all individual products; they are not, as in Diagram 3.1, weighted averages of individual industry supply curves. A fall in domestic costs by a given percentage relative to foreign costs will be represented by a shift in the supply curve from $SS$ to $S^1S^1$. A given percentage fall in the vertical dimension means that the slope of $S^1S^1$ will be less than the slope of $SS$. Accordingly, $EF > BC$, and the maximum burden of protection with the new supply conditions, $DEF$, is greater than $ABC$, the maximum burden under the original supply conditions.

(a) *Increase in Demand.* The analysis of an increase in demand is complicated by the fact that the effects of the constant tariff differ when we start from different initial levels

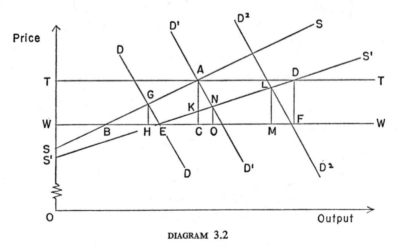

DIAGRAM 3.2

64

of demand. Suppose we start with a demand situation such as
*DD*, where the demand curve crosses the supply curve, *SS*, at
some point between *B* and *A*. Shifts of this curve to the right,
as far as $D^1D^1$, will increase the burden of protection from
*BGH* to *BAC*, and in the standard model will increase the
amount of protection in the same proportion. (The case is
identical to the textbook case of "an increase in a tariff.")
Accordingly, the constant tariff will lead to a fall in both GNP
and GNP per capita growth rates in the standard model. In
the variant model the GNP per capita rate will also fall, but
GNP, and thus the GNP growth rate, will rise as the protected
sector is expanded from *BH* to *BC*, times the population.
Again, the variant model produces a divergence between the
total and per capita growth rates.

If the demand curve then shifts further to the right—or if
we *start* at $D^1D^1$ and shift to the right—the amount of protection will be unchanged, and growth rates unaffected by
comparison with the control situation, since the increased
demand will be satisfied entirely by imports in both cases;
this will be so in both the standard and variant models.

*(b) Decrease in Costs.* The results of a fall in costs will also
depend on the initial demand situation. If the demand curve
intersects *WW* at any point between *B* and *E*, as *DD* does,
the fall in the supply curve to $S^1S^1$ in Diagram 3.2 will wipe
out all protection. Both GNP and GNP per capita in the
standard model will rise by the same amounts as they do in
the control situation since the burden of protection is removed
in both cases; the constant tariff will therefore have no effect
on growth rates. The same conclusion applies to the GNP per
capita rate in the variant model; it also applies to the GNP
rate since production is increased by *HE* per person in both
the constant tariff and control situations. (There will be net
immigration or net emigration in both the actual and control
situations, depending on whether the percentage increase in
output is greater or less than the percentage reduction in
labour requirements per unit of output.)

If the demand curve is $D^2D^2$, so constructed that the
burden of protection after the fall in costs, *LEM*, equals the

burden before the fall in costs, *ABC*, the constant tariff (as distinct from the fall in costs) will leave both the GNP per capita and GNP growth rates unaffected in the standard model. In the control situation, however, both rates would have risen since the burden of protection would have been reduced from *ABC* to *KEC*; the increase in manufactured goods actually produced, *CM* per person, would have been satisfied by imports. The constant tariff therefore reduces both growth rates in the standard model as compared with the control situation. The same conclusion applies to the GNP per capita rate in the variant model. GNP will rise with the constant tariff owing to the increase of (*EM–BC*) per person in protected output, whereas protected output would have fallen from *BC* to *EC* per person in the control situation. The effect of the constant tariff in the variant model is therefore again to increase the GNP growth rate, and again to create divergence between it and the GNP per capita growth rate.

Other cases may be treated summarily since our conclusions have already established a repetitive pattern. If the demand curve lies between *DD* and $D^2D^2$ the burden of protection will fall as the result of the fall in costs, but the rise of new import-replacing, protected, industries will keep it from falling as much as it would have fallen in the control situation. With the demand curve $D^1D^1$ for example, the burden will fall from *ABC* to *NEO*, but in the control situation it would have fallen to *KEC*, with imports rising from zero to *CO*. The constant tariff will prevent all growth rates from rising as far as they otherwise would have risen, except that the GNP rate in the variant model rises farther as a result of factor immigration due to the newly protected output, *CO* times the population. If the demand curve lies to the right of $D^2D^2$, the burden of protection will be increased from *ABC* up to its maximum of *DEF*, and the fall in costs will reduce growth rates absolutely as well as relatively, again with the exception of the GNP rate in the variant model. The conclusions to be drawn from the "increasing costs" case are thus substantially the same as those that were drawn from the "constant costs" analysis; with two exceptions, a constant tariff always reduces growth rates in the economy when the standard model is assumed, and always raises the GNP rate and reduces the GNP per capita rate when the variant model is utilized. In the two exceptional cases the constant tariff has no effect whatever on growth rates. One of these cases is important because it is common: when the original demand curve lies to the right of $D^1D^1$— as it normally will, since there will usually be some imports over the tariff—increases in demand have no effect on the burden or amount of protection since the whole increase in the amount demanded is satisfied by imports. The other exception is rare; for demand curves to the left of $DD$ a fall in costs will wipe out protection completely and render the tariff ineffective.

3. GENERAL SUMMARY

What a constant tariff does is always to keep the size of the protected sector larger than it would have been if the initial "impact effect" of the imposition of the tariff had been its final effect. A constant tariff stands as a constant invitation to the establishment of new, uneconomic, import-replacing industries whenever reductions in costs reduce the burden of currently protected industries, and to the extension of protected industries whenever (in the constant costs case) the demand for protected output increases. Import-replacing industries that need protection are the bane of the consumer, yet the darling of governments, which often seem to desire a large manufacturing sector as an end in itself. Governments, indeed, often seem to display a preference for quantity over quality; in our variant model the constant tariff has been shown to increase the size of the economy, as measured by GNP, even while it reduces the quality of economic life, as measured by GNP per capita.[10] And yet the downward pressure exerted on the standard of living by a constant tariff results from what should be basic growth conditions— increases in demand, and decreases in costs that are *relative*

[10]We have stressed throughout the conclusion that the GNP and GNP per capita rates will diverge by comparison with these rates in the control economy. Such divergence is displayed in Chart 6.1 where the American economy is used as the "control" for the Canadian economy.

to decreases in costs abroad! The only way consumers in a constant tariff economy can be relieved of their burden of protection—assuming that they cannot find a government that *wants* to reduce it—is by some conjuncture of circumstances that will reduce the size of the protected sector of the economy. Citizens of a protected economy should pray for steeply rising excess costs of protected production, economic retrogression in the protected sector (i.e., cost *increases* relative to the rest of the world), and a reduced demand for protected output; for only in these ways can the size of the protected sector be reduced. The constant tariff economy is indeed a topsy-turvy world, a classic case of economic pathology.


## IV

I turn now to a brief discussion of some of the general equilibrium implications of the tendency of a protected sector to grow larger and larger under the aegis of a constant tariff. The analysis deals only with "standard model" situations in which factor supplies are fixed, and even in the cases considered the treatment is far from exhaustive. The truth of the matter is that an adequate statement of the effects of a constant tariff in a general equilibrium setting is well beyond my analytical capabilities, and I only hope that the deficiencies of this section of the paper will encourage someone to do the job properly.

I define my problem as that of showing how the protected sector in a constant tariff economy can be expanded without involving disequilibrium in the balance of payments under a fixed exchange rate.

An increase in demand for protected production—which, as was noted earlier, must come from the domestic economy —raises no special problem in either "constant costs" or "increasing costs" situations when the industries involved are not "working up to the tariff," i.e., when their costs of production, and therefore their prices, are less than world prices plus the tariff. The new demand leads to a shift of domestic resources to the protected sector; and the balance of payments is unaffected, provided that the resources are taken from some sector other than the export sector—for example, the service sector. Income per capita will be reduced by a rise of prices in the sector that has lost resources and in protected industries subject to "increasing costs," but the main loss is likely to be in terms of the real income foregone through the purchasing of domestic goods at prices in excess of world prices. The GNP per capita growth rate, measured at world prices, will be lower than it would have been if the new demand had been directed to some unprotected sector of the economy.

When "increasing costs" industries are "working up to the tariff"—and this will be true whenever part of the domestic market for a protected good is satisfied by imports—an increase in demand for protected products has quite different effects. In Diagram 3.2 it appeared that an increase in demand in these circumstances would be met entirely by increased imports, but in a general equilibrium context partial equilibrium appearances may be deceptive. Imports will increase initially, and the balance of payments will thereby be thrown out of equilibrium. With a fixed exchange rate, correction of this problem will require a policy of domestic deflation. In the protected sector, as costs and prices are forced down, a margin of unutilized protection will develop. Accordingly resources will be drawn into this sector and import-replacing output will expand. At the same time, the deflationary pressure will itself tend to reduce imports and increase exports through its effect on the terms of trade; but this effect is temporary, since the deflationary pressure must sooner or later be removed and goods prices will return to their former levels. In the new equilibrium, however, the factorial terms of trade will have been permanently reduced; to wipe out the initial increase in imports the new import-replacing industries must be maintained, and with a constant tariff (which sets an upper limit to the prices of their products) they can only be maintained by factor prices that are lower in the new equilibrium than they were originally, before the increase in demand for protected products developed. In the new setting, imports will have been reduced from their temporarily high level following the initial increase in demand by the advent of the new import-replacing production and by the fall in money incomes; their new equilibrium level may be, but need not be, lower than their old equilibrium level. Exports will be adjusted to the new level of imports by some balance between the tendency to increase exports resulting from the lower factorial terms of trade and the tendency to reduce them by shifting factors from the export sector to the protected sector.

The rather startling conclusion from this analysis is that when there is an increase in demand for the output of protected industries that are already "working up to the tariff" a constant tariff will nevertheless lead to an expansion of the protected sector, and will ensure this outcome by reducing the money incomes of factors of production.[11] In the traditional analysis of the *imposition* of a tariff, the protected sector is established, and per capita income reduced, by an increase of product prices with unchanged factor prices. The *continuation* of a tariff, we have shown, will under certain not uncommon conditions lead to the expansion of the protected sector, and a further reduction in per capita income, by leading to reduced factor prices with unchanged product prices.

In the case just analysed an *increase* in demand leads to a *fall* of the $SS$ curve in Diagram 3.2 as a result of a reduction in domestic factor prices relative to foreign factor prices. In this respect, the case is similar to the situation analysed in section III where the $SS$ curve fell because of an improvement in productivity in protected industries relative to productivity in the same industries abroad. In the general equilibrium context, however, the expansion of the protected sector under the incentive of relative productivity improvement reduces imports and poses the question of how exports are reduced to restore a balance of payments equilibrium. A possible answer

[11]Under the conditions of the variant model used in section III the interest rate would remain unchanged and the whole brunt of reduced factor incomes would be borne by money wages. Analysis of the reactions to the consequent change in domestic factor-price ratios is not attempted here; but see n. 13.

is that resources to expand the protected sector are withdrawn from the export sector. The reduction in per capita income implicit in the switch is relative rather than absolute; part or all of the increase in income inherent in the relatively improved productivity is spent on the excess costs of newly protected production rather than on imports at world prices. In a rational world a relative productivity improvement in manufacturing would normally lead to increased incomes, increased exports, and increased imports. In a constant tariff economy a relative productivity improvement in protected manufacturing leads to reduced imports, reduced exports, and to either no increase in income or at best an increase that is less than the productivity improvement should have produced.

By assuming a fixed exchange rate, I have so far neglected depreciation of the domestic currency as a possible route to equilibrium when the size of the protected sector is expanded in a constant tariff economy. Depreciation fulfils one condition for the re-establishment of equilibrium; it reduces per capita income by producing a deterioration in the terms of trade. It also tends to satisfy the second condition, an expansion of the protected sector, by tending to increase the *de facto* rate of protection afforded by a given tariff. Its effectiveness in this department, however, depends on the existence of a particular pattern of lags in which the domestic prices of protected goods rise in advance of factor prices. I have ignored depreciation as a possible means of restoring equilibrium in a constant tariff economy because of its questionable effectiveness in a long-run equilibrium analysis. In the real world, though, forces that lead to an expansion of the protected sector may also lead to depreciation, and the pattern of lags in the real world may be such that depreciation serves as an equilibrating mechanism not only in the short run but also in the long run. So much is suggested, in any event, by the recurrent exchange crises[12] and the morbid preoccupation with the so-called "balance of payments" problem in both

[12]"Alterations of the [Canadian] exchange rate [have] . . . occurred nine times since 1918, or about twice per decade." Rudolf R. Rhomberg, "A Model of the Canadian Economy," *Journal of Political Economy*, February, 1964, p. 1.

Canada and Great Britain, two countries where the protected sector of the economy is probably large.

This section then gives us additional reasons for concluding, as we concluded in section III, that "a constant tariff economy is indeed a topsy-turvy world, a classic case of economic pathology." A new tariff lowers a nation's standard of living; even when the passage of time removes the original injury, or at least reduces its relative importance, perpetuation of the tariff serves continually to add new insults and thereby to keep the standard of living continuously lower than it might be. Growth forces in an economy that would normally lead to a higher standard of living by means of a larger volume of international exchange—both exports and imports—become "balance of payments" problems in a protected economy, and a constant tariff works continuously to convert part of the potential gain in the standard of living into a larger protected sector by producing upward pressures on product prices, downward pressures on factor prices,[13] and perhaps, when these mechanisms do not work smoothly enough, by fostering recurrent depreciations. The electorate in a protected country pays continuously for the timidity of politicians in matters of tariff reform.

## APPENDIX

SHIFT EFFECTS

An old argument for protectionism contends that an increase in protection increases GNP (and GNP per capita) by transferring labour (and other factors) from "low-productivity" agriculture to "high-productivity" manufacturing, and that this gain ought to be offset against the loss resulting from the excess costs of protected produc-

[13]Factor-price ratios will be changed if the fall in prices is uneven; no attempt is made here to examine the possible changes and their repercussions. However, as was noted in n. 11, wages will fall relatively to the interest rate in the variant model. A constant tariff tends to cheapen labour in terms of capital. Salter showed that this process reduces "the standards of obsolescence" in an economy and reduces the ratio of "best practice plant" to total plant in all industries in the economy. If Salter's suggestion that economic progress may be correlated to capital-intensive production be correct, a constant tariff would always keep a protected economy a step behind the leaders in economic progress. See W. E. G. Salter, *Productivity and Technical Change* (Cambridge, 1960), *passim*.

tion. Modern measures of GNP lend a certain credibility to this argument, for as high-wage sectors of an economy grow relatively to low-wage sectors a statistical "shift effect" adds to GNP, and in many cases is an important part of measured increases in GNP and GNP per capita. Nevertheless, in long-run equilibrium, units of the same factor of production must earn the same income in all employments, and the "shift effect," in the sense of a mere transfer of units of a given factor from one employment to another, can play no part in increasing real income. In so far as calculated income differentials reflect something more than a disequilibrium situation they are in part statistical artifacts and in part nothing more than a measure of increases in the quality of the labour force.

National accounting conventions include in an urban worker's income many items that may perhaps be called collectively "the costs of employment"— for example, such things as transportation and clothing expenditures associated with urban employment—and that might better, perhaps, be reckoned as intermediate inputs rather than final outputs. In any event many of the analogous items *are* counted as intermediate inputs in calculating the net income of the farm sector, and the result is that national accounts overstate urban incomes relative to rural incomes.

Sectoral income differences that remain after allowance is made for this overstatement represent quality differentials. A useful way to make this point is to say that the excess of incomes in a high-wage sector over those in a low-wage sector represents a return on the excess of the stock of human capital per worker in the former sector over that in the latter.[14] In brief, a farmer cannot raise his income merely by *moving* to the city; he must increase his personal stock of human capital *en route*. It is the *investment*, not the *transfer* (whether tariff-induced or not), that raises GNP.

The income measure used in the text therefore stands; an increase in the amount of protection reduces GNP, and therefore the growth rate. If a positive "shift effect" is associated with an extension of protected production it will have resulted partly from the conventions of national income accounting and partly from increased investment in human capital; in neither case does it obviate the increase in economic cost inherent in an expansion of protected output.

[14]See H. G. Johnson, "The Political Economy of Opulence," *Canadian Journal of Economics and Political Science*, November, 1960, pp. 552–64, esp. pp. 561–3; also, by the same author, "Economics and Politics of Opulence" in *University of Toronto Quarterly*, July, 1965, pp. 313–31, *passim*.

# II

# 4

## Comparing the Canadian and American Economies

In this Part we try to find out what effects, if any, the Canadian tariff has had on the growth of the Canadian economy. We are told that we must design a factual study that is based primarily on historical statistics. Is the project feasible? The answer is surely "no" if we confine our attention to the historical statistics of Canada, for very little can be learned by studying a thing in terms of itself; we should learn very little about elephants from their statistics unless we had statistics for other mammals with which to compare them.

Thus any attempt to design a factual, statistical study of the effects of protection on economic growth immediately runs into serious methodological problems. Ordinarily time-series analysis is quite impossible because the statistics themselves incorporate the effect we want to study—the impact of protection on economic growth—and there is no way of removing it from the data. (To remove it we would have to know what it was—which is what we want to discover!) And yet any study of growth experience must be a study of variables through time.

Cross-sectional analysis is a feasible alternative to time series analysis when some problem in partial equilibrium analysis is involved, for observations can then be collected from many subunits of a single economy. In a study such as ours, however, when what is in question is the general equilibrium of a whole economy, the units in a cross-section analysis would have to be national economies, and as Professor Parker has warned ". . . in a comparison of trends occurring . . . in different social environments, the number of variables is (usually) so large relative to the number of cases, that the conditions for a satisfactory explanation can hardly be met."[1] And so to comparative history.

## I

"Comparative history" is not a very well defined term, and its intellectual respectability as a research method is not well established. The term itself implies some combination of comparisons through space and comparisons through time—some combination of cross-sectional analysis and time series analysis. In practice the cross-sectional component is usually rudimentary since, if we except Toynbee, the through-space comparison is usually confined to two or three countries. Indeed the comparative method may best be thought of as a cross-sectional analysis based on only a few (say, two or three) items. Can anything be learned from a comparison of two cases? In principle at least, the answer must be "yes." If we observe two different entities, and are then told that all their attributes save one are common to both of them, we are willing to conclude that the difference in the entities is caused by the difference in the one attribute. As the number of attributes that differ between the two terms of the comparison increases, our ability to identify the cause of the observed difference in the entities becomes weaker and weaker. Still, so long as the number of differences is small, and the ratio of similarities to differences is large, some understanding can be gained; the number of admissible explanations of the difference in the entities is confined to the small number of differences in attributes, and the comparison has at least ruled out the large

[1]W. N. Parker, "Introduction" to *Trends in the American Economy in the Nineteenth Century* (National Bureau of Economic Research, Studies in Income and Wealth, vol. 24; Princeton, 1960), p. 7. Exactly the same comment is appropriate to comparisons through time in one country, the basis of "normal" history, for the social environment varies through time as well as through space. The wonder is that we can ever learn anything—if we can!

number of hypotheses that might have been based on the large number of attributes that are common to the two cases. Moreover, it may be possible to rule out, on logical grounds, some of the "admissible" hypotheses based on differences, and thus still further to reduce the area of our ignorance. Comparison as such, therefore, seems to be a legitimate method of inquiry; the difficulty in applying it is to be satisfied that the comparison is "fair" and "meaningful," i.e., that its two terms in fact differ in only a small number of respects and that their similarities greatly outweigh their differences.

This difficulty is very acute, of course, in comparative history. Parker's comment would seem to be especially compelling when "the number of cases" is reduced to two. And yet the "number of variables" (what we have called the number of differences) will also be reduced when the number of cases is reduced; it is even possible that if the two cases are carefully chosen the former may be reduced in much greater proportion than the latter, and that we may at least approximate the requirements of a "fair" comparison. I shall argue presently that an economic comparison of Canada and the United States is, indeed, fair and meaningful. For the moment I turn to a second difficulty in the application of comparative history.

Comparative *history* implies that similarities between two countries at one time will remain similarities *through* time, so that differences in the historical trends of the countries may be associated with their differences in attributes (which are also assumed to remain differences *through* time). If these assumptions were not met, so that similarities at one time became differences at other times, and *vice versa,* comparative history would indeed become so complicated and unwieldy that it would hardly be worth pursuing. In fact, our confidence in some considerable measure of historical continuity encourages us to believe that important similarities and differences between nations are likely to persist, not indeed indefinitely, but for long enough to permit a useful study of the effects through time of those differences between two countries that have been identified by a number of through-space comparisons, each of which is made at a point in time. Again, the practical problem is one of warranty; to design a study in comparative economic history one must attempt to warrant not only that the comparison is "fair" at one point in time, but also that it will remain "fair" over the time period under consideration.

The basic requirement for using the comparative method is, of course, that the two entities being compared should *differ* in the attribute under investigation (in this case tariff protection) so that one term of the comparison can serve as a "control" for the other. The basic assumption that underlies both this essay and the next two essays is that the American tariff has been "ineffective" over the period (roughly 1890 to 1950) covered by our analysis and that the United States economy during that period has in fact operated on a "free trade" basis.[2] This contention is perhaps ludicrous enough at first sight to require some supporting argument.

Let us begin by noting that a tariff rate is *not* the same thing as a rate of protection. Any given tariff rate may be completely otiose so far as protection is concerned, or it may provide any rate of protection from zero to infinity, i.e., a rate that completely excludes competitive imports. Moreover, a tariff rate that is protective at one time may not be at another, and *vice versa*. The result is that tariff rates are of little significance for the student of protection, and the tariff history of a country provides only the weakest of clues to its history of protection. The question of fact is always whether a given

[2]Similar statements in earlier drafts of this paper aroused reactions ranging all the way from incredulity to disbelief—evidence in itself of the implicit identification of tariff history with the history of protected production. Our argument requires only the weaker contention that Canadian manufacturing has been more highly protected than American manufacturing. Nevertheless F. W. Taussig can be quoted in support of the stronger view. After a discussion of the move to higher duties in the Tariff of 1897, he ventured one of his rare generalizations: "The United States is a great manufacturing country . . . one in which the bulk of the manufacturing industries is no longer seriously dependent on protection. . . . The protective system will be of less and less consequence. . . . [The] absolute effect, still more the proportional effect, of such legislation on the industrial development of the country will diminish. . . . [On] the whole, protective duties, however important they may be in this detail or that, cannot seriously affect the general course of industrial growth, and will affect it less and less as time goes on." F. W. Taussig, *Tariff History of the United States* (8th ed., New York, 1951), pp. 358, 359–60. Taussig never confused tariff history with the history of protection.

80

tariff is *effective*—whether it actually protects—and if so to what extent.

I define an *effective* tariff as one that leads to the establishment of domestic industries that produce at costs in excess of world costs. All other tariffs are *ineffective*: a Canadian tariff on oranges does not lead to the production of oranges in Canada, and is therefore a tax on consumption rather than a subsidy to production; nor would a Canadian tariff on newsprint have any effect on production—the large exports of Canadian newsprint provide sufficient proof that it is produced at or below world costs, *not* at costs above world costs.

The ability to export, in the absence of export subsidization, or some other version of a two-price system,[3] is, indeed, proof of the absence of protection; protected industries, by definition, produce at costs above world costs and therefore cannot export their products. Unfortunately, the reverse proposition is not necessarily true; the absence of exports is not a satisfactory test of protection because industries whose products incur heavy transport costs, though perfectly efficient, may not be able to export because the same industries in foreign markets are "sheltered" by the high transport costs.

Consider, now, the following syllogism. Protected manufacturers cannot export; American manufacturers were, at least during the period from 1890 to 1950, among the world's leading exporters of manufactured goods; therefore American manufacturers during that period were not protected. I realize that both the minor premise and the conclusion are fairly rough statements that cannot be claimed to represent the whole truth and nothing but the truth. Nevertheless, I have enough confidence in the syllogism to contend that the American tariff on manufactured goods during the last two decades of the nineteenth century and the first half of the twentieth century has had little protective effect, and that throughout this period the great bulk of American manufacturing has

---

[3]Some evidence exists that many firms do sell at lower prices in export markets than in home markets, but there is no suggestion that the export prices are unprofitable. See R. E. Caves, *Trade and Economic Structure* (Cambridge, Mass., 1960), p. 281.

therefore operated on a substantially "free trade" basis. That is all I need in order to use the American economy as a "control" for the comparison; if protection is effective in the Canadian economy its effects should show up in the behaviour of some of the Canadian : American series (to be described in the next section) on which the present comparison is based.

## II

Let us now return to the "warranty" of the Canadian-American comparison. In general, the two economies are considered comparable because they are very similar in respect to most of the basic features that underlie the economic organization of a society. The populations of the two countries have similar economic motivations and goals and display similar patterns of tastes; entrepreneurs in both countries make use of similar forms of business organization, employ similar technologies, and are subject to much the same kinds of economic policies pursued by their respective governments. In brief, the "economic environments" of the two countries are strikingly similar. It may also be argued that, since the late 1920s at least, the economic histories of Canada and the United States have been very similar. Occupying the same part of the world, the two countries have been exposed at the same times to economic forces emanating from other parts of the world and, with excellent communications between them, each has been subject almost simultaneously to new technologies, new economic ideas, changes in policies, and shifts in tastes that have arisen in the other. It seems fair to assume, in brief, that the passage of time has affected the two countries in roughly the same ways. Arguing from similarities alone, we should expect the relative position of the two economies through time to be quite stable.

The comparison that is carried out in the next two essays is based on "time series of Canadian : American percentages." Canadian figures for population, gross national product, three categories of output, and various derivatives of these figures, are first expressed as percentages of the corresponding Ameri-

82

can figures for as many years as possible. The percentages for each magnitude are then charted as a time series. Each individual percentage is a through-space comparison at a point in time, and each series is a record of such comparisons through time. An uptrend in a series indicates that Canada is growing more rapidly (or declining less rapidly) than the United States in terms of the magnitude under consideration, and a downtrend that Canada is growing more slowly (or declining more rapidly) than the United States.

Reasoning from similarities alone, we should expect the "time series of percentages" to be quite "flat," with no consistent uptrend or downtrend. A trendless series indicates that, for the economic attribute in question, the *relationship* between the two economies has been reasonably stable through time, even though the percentage changes over time in the attribute in each economy may have been large and fluctuating. This is the sort of outcome that we should surely expect to find in a comparison of two economies so similar as those of Canada and the United States. Our primary expectation, then, is that the series of Canadian : American percentages should be trendless. To put the matter in a different way I claim, rather boldly I know, that the technique of "time series of percentages" substantially eliminates the disturbing effects of time from my comparison. Thus the second basic assumption of the comparison is that *time has had identically proportional effects on the Canadian and American economies during the period considered in the analysis*. To overthrow this assumption it would be necessary to show that time had affected the two economies *differentially*. The argument of the present section has attempted to suggest that it would be difficult to maintain such a contention.


III


Turn now to differences. As I have argued, a large number of similarities is not a sufficient condition for a fair and meaningful comparison; there must also be a small number of differences. And it is in the differences, of course, that we must

83

seek for explanations when the series of Canadian : American percentages do show persistent uptrends or downtrends over time, and are therefore inconsistent with our primary expectation. To illustrate: the actual comparison shows a persistent uptrend in the Canadian : American GNP series, while the GNP per capita series, which shows per capita income in Canada to be about 70 per cent of per capita income in the United States, displays no trend, or perhaps a slight downtrend. This combination of observations poses the basic question to which we seek an answer: *What mechanism is at work to make the Canadian economy grow faster than the American in terms of total national income even though Canadian per capita income remains persistently much below the American?*

The observed behaviour must be explained by the *differences* between the two terms of our comparison. We have already discussed a possible difference concerning the effectiveness of protection in the two countries, though this difference has not yet been established. We shall now discuss other differences between Canada and the United States; each such difference provides a possible hypothesis to answer the problem posed by the data.

If we ignore the host of minor differences between the Canadian and American economies that are either insignificant or are only tenuously related to the problem under consideration, it seems to me that, apart from the possible difference in protection already discussed, there are only two major differences between the two countries with which we need be concerned: a "resource" difference; and a difference in immigration policy. From each of these primary differences there will flow several, perhaps many, observable statistical differences between the two economies, but because these "secondary" differences are derivative (and may therefore be considered aspects of the primary differences) they constitute no barrier to the analysis.

Consider, first, the resource difference; under this term I include such things as differences in natural resource endowment, climate, topography, and the geographical "lay-out" of the two economies. From this resource difference will result several "secondary" differences: a difference in the pattern of production in the two economies; differences in the amounts and types of exports and imports; probable differences in statistical averages for such things as the skill level of the labour force, labour productivity, and the national capital-output ratio; and no doubt many other statistically observable differences. All of these differences will affect the *level* of Canadian:American percentages of such magnitudes as population, income per capita, agricultural production, manufacturing output, and so on; but they will not impart any *trend* to the percentages unless they change differentially over time; and because they are derivative differences their ratios are not likely to change unless the basic resource difference itself changes.

A resource difference is not a static thing despite the fact that it reflects different natural resource endowments. Natural resources can only be defined in terms of technology, and thus technological changes affect relative natural resource endowments; the same technological change, impinging on different natural resource endowments, may well enhance the value of the natural resource capital of one country and depreciate that of another. Actually there is good reason to think that twentieth-century technological changes have favoured Canada relative to the United States, and that therefore changes in the "resource difference" should have made for a long-run *uptrend* in the Canadian : American percentages of various categories of output, of GNP, and of GNP per capita. A number of arguments may be advanced in support of this view.

First, several developments at the end of the nineteenth century, including an important technological change in flour-milling, resulted in the valorization of Western Canada's agricultural resources just at the time of the "closing" of the American frontier. The settlement of Canada's prairie areas provided a strong upward thrust to the Canadian economy until 1920, and a somewhat weaker impulse from 1920 to 1930, at which time the Canadian frontier may also be said to have "closed." Second, and more important in my opinion,

85

is a cluster of arguments relating to technological trends and resource patterns. Strong technological forces favouring differential economic growth in Canada have been apparent both before and since 1930. Paper-making technology and non-ferrous metal-refining technology both favoured Canada over the United States simply because Canada was comparatively "rich" in pulpwood and base metal resources. Much more important was the effect of hydroelectric technology in valorizing waterpower resources, which were again of greater "weight" in the Canadian than in the American resource endowment. To some extent waterpower became a substitute for coal, a strategic industrial resource in which Canada was very weak relative to the United States; at the same time, large and continuous reductions in the amount of fuel required per unit of output over a wide range of production further reduced Canada's relative disadvantage in energy resources. As a result of these two developments Canada's energy base was significantly improved; this improvement, in turn should have favoured differentially rapid growth in several sectors of the Canadian economy, including manufacturing. Moreover, electric drive and the development of truck transport are generally considered, and I think reasonably so, to have reduced the "minimum-optimum" size of plant in many manufacturing industries, and this change should have favoured the growth of a variety of import-competing manufacturing in "small" countries such as Canada.[4] In only one field have technological developments clearly been more advantageous to the United States than to Canada; major advances in agricultural techniques in the production of corn, cotton, soybeans, and rice have been important to American agriculture, but have had little effect in Canada where these crops are either not grown or are grown only in small quantities. The slight decline since 1930 in Canadian agricultural output relative to American, as shown in Chart 6.1, probably reflects this differential impact of agricultural technology. On balance, however, technological trends during the past sixty years have

[4]See J. H. Dales, *Hydroelectricity and Economic Development: Quebec 1898–1940* (Cambridge, Mass., 1957), chap. 8.

clearly favoured the Canadian economy. The "resource difference" has therefore tended to promote more rapid economic growth in Canada than in the United States, and therefore to produce an uptrend in Canadian : American output and income series except in the case of agricultural output.

The second primary difference that affects our comparison is the contrast between Canadian and American immigration policies that has existed since the early 1920s, when American immigration quotas were first introduced. Since that time American immigration policy has severely restricted immigration from most countries by quotas based on nativity; natives of certain Latin American countries and Canada, however, have been exempt from the quota system. In Canada, on the other hand, official policy has always favoured large immigration. Administrative restrictions have been used to reduce immigration during periods of unemployment in Canada (when the number of applicants is in any event reduced) and entry has been encouraged whenever the economy is deemed capable of "absorbing" more workers.[5] One result of the difference in policy is that immigration has been proportionately larger in Canada than it has been in the United States; another is that changes in immigration have been a major component of changes in the labour force in Canada, but not in the United States. Moreover, the combination of immigration policies in the two countries may have had a significant effect on the nativity composition of the Canadian population. Prosperous conditions in North America have tended to bring to Canada large numbers of European immigrants who were excluded from the United States by the quota system; at the same time prosperity in the United States is likely to attract a large number of native Canadians who are not subject to quota. Moreover, because of the much lower standard of living in Canada than in the United States, there tends to be a large emigration of native Canadians to the United States at all times. Recent immigrants from Europe therefore tend to be a larger fraction of the Canadian than the American

[5]See Mabel F. Timlin, *Does Canada Need More People?* (Toronto, 1951), chap. I.

87

population, especially during prolonged periods of prosperity such as the dozen or so years after the Second World War.

The resource difference is a "safety feature" in my subsequent analysis in the sense that it tends to close the gap between the Canadian and American standards of living, while one of my major problems is to explain why in fact the gap has *not* closed; the immigration difference, on the other hand, is an embarrassment since it competes with my main thesis that it is Canadian protectionism that has perpetuated the gap. It is obviously possible that demographic factors, either the immigration difference referred to or a difference in rates of natural increase between Canada and the United States, might explain the large and continuing differential between per capita income in the two countries. Any difference in rates of natural increase would, however, offer only a very weak hypothesis to account for the observation, for the uninhibited flow of Americans and native-born Canadians across the border should prevent any large income gap from developing for this reason. It is quite otherwise in the case of the immigration difference because, as noted, many immigrants to Canada have been ineligible to enter the United States. Differential immigration therefore *could* explain both the opening of the income gap and its maintenance. However, I reject the immigration hypothesis as a sufficient explanation of the problem, if only because Canadian immigration policy has *not* allowed immigrants to enter the country so freely that they normally arrive *before* there are jobs available for them; in administering the policy an attempt has naturally been made to avoid any situation in which immigrants would have to create their own job opportunities by bidding down the price of labour in Canada. Had this been the mechanism at work, the income gap between Canada and the United States would no doubt be much greater than it actually is.

But while I reject the immigration difference as a sufficient explanation for the persistence of the observed income gap, there is no doubt that it is a necessary part of the explanation. As will become apparent, my main explanatory hypothesis is based on the difference in protection that is identified in the following chapter; the immigration difference is assigned a subsidiary role in the argument. In brief, the Canadian tariff is seen as the "dynamic" factor in the situation: effective protectionism in Canada tends continuously to create more job opportunities at the current money wage than would otherwise have developed; and the resulting excess demand for labour is satisfied by a "passive" inflow of immigrants.

It will no doubt have been observed that nothing has yet been said about economies of scale, the favourite Canadian explanation of any and all observed inefficiencies in the Canadian economy. Since the topic will be discussed in the final essay in the volume little need be said about it here. It may simply be noted in passing that arguments from economies of scale that point to the great absolute difference in the size of the Canadian and American economies as a relevant factor in explaining the per capita income gap between the two countries serve, like the "resource" difference, as a safety factor in our analysis. At any time in the past, Canada must be presumed to have had more unexhausted economies of scale than the United States, and with growth in both countries—more especially with greater growth of population and GNP in Canada than in the United States—Canada should therefore have harvested more such economies than the United States. Thus whenever the data show that income per capita in Canada has grown less rapidly, or no more rapidly, than in the United States we can be reasonably sure that this observation cannot be explained by differences in "technology" or "the economies of scale" between the two countries; these things should have tended to *close* the income gap between Canada and the United States.

IV

In summary, I have tried in this essay to argue that comparative history, even when only two countries are involved, is a useful, if treacherous, intellectual strategy. By means of comparison it is possible to learn some things about a country that could not be known by a study of that country alone. The reason is that time is irreversible and will not perform *ceteris paribus* experiments for us; what I have argued is that a comparison that can be warranted "fair" is in fact capable of holding both time and a lot of other things constant, and thus of isolating a few factors for study in a simulated environment of "comparative statics."

The treacherousness of the strategy lies, of course, in the fact that the person who uses it can never be sure that he has recognized *all* the differences between the terms of his comparison. And because the hypothesis adduced to explain the observations originate in these differences, it is always possible that the true explanation of the observations lies somewhere among the differences that the investigator has overlooked rather than among those he has identified. A comparative technique is always "open-ended" in this sense, and each comparison must be accepted or rejected on its own merits. But the method as such cannot be cavalierly discarded on the grounds that no comparison is ever perfect, any more than the deductive method in economics can be cavalierly rejected on the grounds that its assumptions never represent the facts of a case with complete accuracy. In the final analysis, all forms of intellectual enquiry are essays in persuasion.

The second purpose of this chapter has been to describe the technique used in the particular Canadian-American comparison with which the next two chapters are concerned, and to outline the intellectual strategy that is involved in drawing conclusions from the comparison. It will be well to repeat here the two basic assumptions, developed in this chapter, that underlie the argument of the following two essays: (1) the American tariff was ineffective, and American manufacturers produced under substantially free trade conditions, during the period covered by the analysis; and (2) time has affected the Canadian and American economies in the same ways and in strict proportion to their sizes, except in respect to the three differences between them that have been identified: the protection difference; the resource difference; and the immigration difference.

# 5

## Canadian Protection in American Perspective

### *A Statistical Enquiry*

Has manufacturing in Canada been protected? The importance assigned to the tariff in writings on Canadian economic history makes the question seem prissily academic until we remember that any given *tariff* rate may result in any rate of *protection* from zero to infinity (i.e., a rate that completely excludes imports). It then becomes clear that our question is a member of a whole genus of questions that pose one of the most important, and most intractable, problems in economic history: to what extent, if at all, do governmental economic policies affect economic trends? All too often the intent of economic legislation is confidently taken to bear a one-to-one relationship to its effect, and one shudders to think how much that passes for economic history has been based on this frail assumption.

The purpose of the present essay is to test the hypothesis that the Canadian tariff has been protective in fact. Before the tariff can be declared effective two propositions must be established. First, it must be shown that the sector of the economy that is "protected" suffers from a comparative disadvantage; if the sector in question enjoyed a comparative advantage, the tariff would be redundant by definition. Second, since it is theoretically possible that the Canadian manufacturing statistics on which the first demonstration is based are the statistics of sheltered output rather than protected output (and that the test therefore only demonstrates comparative disadvantage at zero transport costs), it must be shown that the costs of domestic output exceed world costs plus transport costs. Only if the evidence supports both propositions will we be able to argue with some assurance that the Canadian tariff has actually done what it was intended to do, namely, distort the Canadian economy. And as will be seen, it is not easy to prove what is normally taken for granted.

The method used in the essay has been described in the previous essay. American experience is taken as a "free trade" standard against which to compare Canadian experience. The data are presented in various "time series of Canadian : American percentages," and conclusions are drawn from both the relative levels and the relative time trends displayed by different series.

### I. COMPARATIVE ADVANTAGE

If the Canadian tariff has been effective relative to the American tariff (which we have argued has been ineffective on average), it will have promoted the development in Canada of manufacturing industries in which Canada has a comparative disadvantage with respect to the United States. To test for the existence of such a comparative disadvantage requires an indirect procedure and a major "labour-cost" assumption whose credentials must be examined.

The test is conducted on two large economic aggregates in each economy. The manufacturing sector in Canada, the allegedly protected sector, is taken to be secondary manufacturing[1]; figures for this sector are compared to figures for *all* manufacturing in the United States. The residual sector is the rest of the non-agricultural economy; in Canada it is the total economy less agriculture and secondary manufacturing, and in the United States it is the total economy less agriculture and all manufacturing.

As background for the analysis it will be well to keep in

[1]See the statistical appendix to chapter 6 for definitions of concepts, sources of data, and estimating procedures used.

mind two major presumptions that underlie the argument not only of this chapter but of the volume as a whole. One is the assumption that production functions, in the sense of the knowledge of all technically feasible production possibilities, are the same in all countries. The second is the generalization, based on historical experience, that wages in Canada are below wages in the United States while interest rates in Canada are above those in the United States; accordingly, for the same output of the same product, more labour and less capital will normally be used in Canada than in the United States.

Like other tests for comparative advantage, mine depends ultimately on the assumption that the ratio of the costs of production of the same commodity in the two countries (and thus the ratio of prices of the commodity in the two countries since we assume competitive pricing, i.e., that price equals the cost of production in each country) is equal to the ratio of unit labour costs (the wage times the reciprocal of labour productivity) in the two countries. We are constrained, therefore, to make use of a modified labour theory of value in which international price ratios are equal to (though not, I think, necessarily caused by) international ratios of labour costs per unit of output.[2] It is worth noting that the constraint results not from any analytical necessity, but purely from the

[2]The argument on which the test is based is essentially the same as that used by G. D. A. MacDougall, "British and American Exports," *Economic Journal*, December, 1951, pp. 697–724. J. Bhagwati in "The Pure Theory of International Trade," *Economic Journal*, March, 1964, pp. 1–84, argues that MacDougall's (and others') work "has little to do with the empirical verification of the Ricardian hypothesis" (p. 12), and that the lack of significant correlation between international productivity ratios and export price ratios makes it impossible to forecast export-import patterns from productivity ratios (p. 17). Bhagwati's demonstration of the lack of correlation is based on individual industry data; perhaps the use of sectoral aggregates in the present chapter results in making some provision for *indirect* labour productivities, the lack of which in individual industry data is one of the deficiencies of a test of the Ricardian theory based on industries (p. 14). In this connection see also a comment by S. F. Kaliski in the *Canadian Journal of Economics and Political Science*, November, 1964, p. 637, in a book review of R. E. Lipsey, *Price and Quantity Trends in the Foreign Trade of the United States* (Princeton, 1963). In my own use of the MacDougall method I am seeking neither to verify the Ricardian hypothesis (I *assume* it) nor to explain (or forecast) export-import patterns; I am attempting to detect the presence or absence of comparative advantage in different sectors as between Canada and the United States. A hypothesis which may be too crude for one purpose may be satisfactory for another.

93

absence of complete cost data. We have rough data for labour costs, some data on capital costs that are both unreliable and very difficult to interpret, and almost no information at all on other costs. If we had complete cost data, of course, there would be no need to be so devious in testing for comparative advantage; a simple comparison of the national "costs of production" for the commodity in question, suitably adjusted for the exchange rate, would do the trick. But in the present state of information we must use labour cost data alone or admit that comparative advantage is a non-operational concept. I do not want to prejudge the issue, and I do not accept the plausible argument that a "good try" is always better than nothing. It does seem to me, however, that in the present case a "labour-cost proxy" for international cost ratios *is* better than nothing, if only because labour costs constitute, on average, something like 70 per cent of total costs of production in *both* the United States and Canada. Moreover, simply because labour costs are a large proportion of total costs *on the average*, a ratio of labour costs is likely to be a better proxy for the required ratio of total costs (prices) when the proxy refers to large economic aggregates than if the units under consideration are individual industries.

The particular form of the general "labour-cost" assumption that is required for the present analysis is that the Canadian : American ratio of *average* labour costs of production should be equal to the Canadian : American ratio of the *marginal* labour costs of production. The well-known equation stating that the wage rate in any unit of production equals the marginal productivity of labour times the price of the product implies that the ratio of Canadian : American prices for the same product will equal the ratio of the Canadian : American wage rates divided by the ratio of the Canadian : American marginal productivities of labour. The trouble, of course, is that we have no figures for the marginal productivity of labour in either Canada or the United States: hence my assumption that the required ratio equals the ratio of *average* productivities of labour, for which we *do* have figures.

It would be difficult to construct a compelling argument either for or against this assumption. For any given "pair" of

94

marginal and average productivities in the United States there will be an infinite number of "production points" in Canada that would justify the assumption, and an infinite number that would invalidate it. In the end whatever confidence one places in the assumption must derive from the confidence he places in the general comparison of the Canadian and American economies. In its defence I appeal simply to the similarity of production techniques in the two countries, and to the view developed in chapter 4 that shifts in production techniques in one country are likely to be quickly matched by similar shifts in the other.

Let the capital letters $P$, $M$, and $W$, stand for the price of output, the marginal physical productivity of labour, and money wages, respectively, and let the miniscules $c$, $a$, $m$, and $r$ be used as subscripts to represent Canada, the United States, manufacturing output, and "residual" output. The hypothesis is that manufacturing in Canada suffers a comparative disadvantage, i.e., that

$$Pmc/Prc > Pma/Pra$$
$$\text{or that}$$
$$Pmc/Pma > Prc/Pra.$$

In order that one country shall not import both (groups of) goods it is also necessary that the left-hand term be greater than 1, and the right-hand term less than 1. When the $P$'s are interpreted to mean hypothetical costs (prices) before trade, the opening of trade would lead to complete specialization of $c$ in $r$, and of $a$ in $m$.

When there is incomplete specialization the $P$'s refer to actual costs (prices), and the inequality in the comparative advantage expression results in part from transport costs; at the margin, with trade, the prices of $r$ and $m$, allowing for transport costs, must be the same in both countries. In order that $r$ may be exported from $c$ to $a$, the average costs of producing $r$ in $c$ at a level of output in excess of domestic requirements must be lower than the average costs of producing import requirements in $a$ by at least the cost of shipping $r$ from $c$ to $a$; similarly, the opposite must be true for the costs of producing $m$ in the two countries. The condition that one country must not have a comparative advantage in both goods must also be restated to read that the left-hand side of the inequalities must be greater than the exchange rate[3] $e$ between the two countries, or that $Pmc/Pma > e$ and that $Prc/Pra < e$.

In equilibrium, the well-known relationships between $P$, $W$, and $M$ are as follows:

$$Pmc = Wmc/Mmc; \quad Prc = Wrc/Mrc;$$
$$Pma = Wma/Mma; \quad Pra = Wra/Mra.$$

The hypothesis about comparative advantage is therefore

$$\frac{Wmc}{Wma} \cdot \frac{Mma}{Mmc} > e < \frac{Wrc}{Wra} \cdot \frac{Mra}{Mrc}$$

$$\text{or } \frac{1}{e}\frac{Wmc}{Wma} > \frac{Mmc}{Mma}, \quad \text{and} \quad \frac{1}{e}\frac{Wrc}{Wra} < \frac{Mrc}{Mra}.$$

Since we accept the ratio of *average* labour productivities as a proxy for the ratio of *marginal* labour productivities, it follows that if Canada displays a comparative disadvantage with respect to the United States in $m$, and a comparative advantage in $r$, observations of relative wages in the manufacturing sectors of Canada and the United States (adjusted by the exchange rate) should lie above observations of relative labour productivities in the manufacturing sectors of the two countries; and that the reverse should be true in the residual sectors.

The crudity of the experiment should be emphasized. Its

---

[3]The data in charts 5.1 and 5.2 are adjusted by the average level of the exchange rate in each year. This procedure is followed because it biases the results in a conservative direction, i.e., the results are "worse" than if no exchange rate adjustment were made. (See n. 5 below.) How a change in the general exchange rate affects prices and costs in particular sectors, and with what lag, is unknown. Since our sectors are very large aggregates it would probably have been justifiable to ignore the exchange rate and follow the Economic Council of Canada's procedure in a similar comparison of assuming that "the differences in the levels of prices are taken . . . to reflect any effects of the exchange rate on the domestic price levels. . . ." Economic Council of Canada, *Second Annual Review* (Ottawa, 1966), p. 54.

units are large economic aggregates; and the measurements employed are rough statistical averages such as "annual earnings per worker" and "annual output (in constant dollars) per worker." Chaotic results would hardly be astonishing. Nevertheless, the linkages between the Canadian and American economies are so strong that Canadian : American percentages should display considerable stability in "normal" periods and be reasonably sensitive to "abnormal" economic movements that affect one economy but not the other. Moreover, the ruggedness of the economic linkage between labour productivity, output, costs, and prices that is displayed at the industry level[4] suggests that these relationships may also be statistically apparent even at a highly aggregative level of analysis.

In fact, as Charts 5.1 and 5.2 show, the statistical results display surprising conformity with the hypothesis. In both charts the $M$ curves are the Canadian : American percentages for labour productivity, and the $W$ curves the Canadian : American percentages for wages (annual earnings). In Chart 5.1, manufacturing, the $W$ Curve (adjusted for the exchange rate) lies above the $M$ curve in nineteen of twenty-four observations[5]; in Chart 5.2 the residual sector, the $W$ curve (adjusted for the exchange rate) lies below the $M$ curve in all cases. The results seem suspiciously good; yet I have been unable to think of any reason why they might merely represent "statistical artifacts."[6] I therefore take them as they stand and suggest that they provide strong support for the hypothesis that Canada experiences a comparative disadvantage in manufacturing with respect to the United States.

One final point. Some will argue that Canada's comparative disadvantage in manufacturing is perfectly obvious from the

[4]See W. E. G. Salter, *Productivity and Technical Change* (Cambridge, 1960), esp. pp. 124 and 166–9.
[5]Two of the exceptions, 1950 and 1951, result from the exchange rate adjustment. Since some of the effects of the exchange depreciation of September 19, 1949, were probably absorbed by profit margins, our procedure no doubt lowers the $W$ curve unduly.
[6]For those who are suspicious of statisticians rather than of statistics, it may be of interest to know that this article was written backwards; the charts were drawn, and the "test" therefore made, almost a year before the "experiment" was formulated!

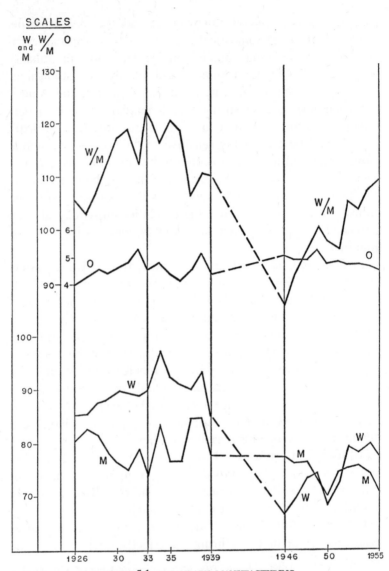

CHART 5.1. SECONDARY MANUFACTURING

(Canadian data for secondary manufacturing as percentages of United States data for all manufacturing)

O    = Output (constant dollars)
M    = Output per employed worker (constant dollars)
W    = Earnings per employee (current dollars)
W/M = Labour costs per unit of output (current dollars)

98

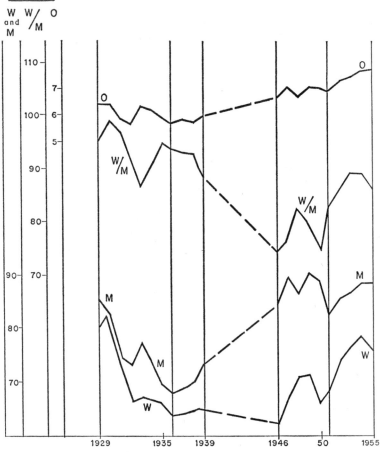

CHART 5.2. THE RESIDUAL SECTOR
(Canadian data for the whole economy excluding agriculture and secondary
manufacturing as percentages of United States data for the whole economy
excluding agriculture and all manufacturing)
O    = Output (constant dollars)
M    = Output per employed worker (constant dollars)
W    = Earnings per employee (current dollars)
W/M = Labour costs per unit of output (current dollars)

well-known fact of Canada's persistently "unfavourable"
balance of trade in manufactured goods, and that any statistical demonstration of the obvious is a waste of time. My

reply would be that the exercise is not *entirely* a waste of time; if the fact of comparative advantage is claimed to be obvious, it is gratifying that the test does not deny the obvious; and the fact that it does not serves in some degree both to support the reliability of the data and to validate the method used. Others will argue that it is impossible confidently to infer the existence of comparative advantage, or disadvantage, from trade flows alone, on the grounds that money prices, on which trade flows depend, are subject to so many monopolistic and institutional distortions that they do not accurately reflect real costs and "true" comparative advantage. This is the point of view implicitly adopted in the above test; it seeks to establish the "true" state of comparative advantage since the analysis runs not in terms of prices but of costs—labour costs, in both money and physical terms.

## II. EFFECTIVE PROTECTION

The conclusion that Canada experiences a comparative disadvantage in manufacturing does not mean that the Canadian tariff has been effective. The different relative positions of the *M* and *W* curves in Charts 5.1 and 5.2 may simply reflect the impact of transport costs in a situation of incomplete specialization. If this were so the data of Chart 5.1 would depict an equilibrium situation, and there would be no presumption that the level of Canadian manufacturing output had been inflated by the tariff. I shall argue, however, that the gap between the *M* and *W* curves in Chart 5.1 cannot be explained by transport costs alone, and that it in fact also reflects the existence of high-cost manufacturing production that has developed in Canada because of the tariff and despite Canada's comparative disadvantage in manufacturing. I shall also argue that many of the other characteristics of Charts 5.1 and 5.2 give further support to the hypothesis that Canadian manufacturing has been highly protected relative to American manufacturing.

The analysis is facilitated by adding two series to Charts

100

5.1 and 5.2: Canadian : American percentages of output in constant dollars (the $O$ series); and the $W/M$ series. The latter represents "relative money labour costs per unit of output," and on the basis of the assumption used in the preceding section we interpret it as a proxy for "relative money costs (prices) of output." The *trend* of the $W/M$ series should serve as a good indicator of the *trend* of relative costs (prices) of output. Part of the argument that follows, however, depends on the assumption that the *level* of the $W/M$ series is a good measure of the level of relative prices. This assumption is part and parcel of the general "labour-costs" assumption. Obviously the $W/M$ series will be an accurate measure of relative costs of production if non-labour costs per unit of output in the two countries are strictly proportional to the ratio of unit labour costs; if the Canadian : American ratio of unit non-labour costs exceeds the ratio of unit labour costs the level of the $W/M$ series will *understate* the true ratio of costs of production, and *vice versa*. Lack of information prevents our knowing whether, on average, the $W/M$ series as a measure of relative prices is biased upward or downward.

The argument is presented in three parts.

1. THE EXCESS OF CANADIAN COSTS (PRICES)

The $W/M$ curve always lies above the 100 per cent level when relative money wages exceed relative productivities; and always lies below 100 per cent when the $M$ curve exceeds the $W$ curve. In the 1930s money labour costs per unit of manufacturing output averaged about 15 per cent above the corresponding American figures, while in the 1950s the excess of Canadian over American costs was only 5 or 6 per cent. Changing levels of the $W/M$ curve in Chart 5.1 have been determined mainly by trends in the $W$ curve, whose average level has varied over time much more than the average level of the $M$ curve. The question then arises whether, from the point of view of "long-run equilibrium," the $W/M$ curve was abnormally high in the 1930s, when the $W$ curve was far above the $M$ curve, or abnormally low in

101

the 1950s, when the $W$ and $M$ curves were much closer together. On our assumption about the similarity of trends in Canadian and American production techniques, theory suggests that the $W/M$ curve was high in the 1930s; if over time Canadian productivity is reasonably steady at about $x$ per cent of American productivity Canadian wages sought also to be reasonably steady at about $x$ per cent of American wages. The suggestion that the $W$ curve was abnormally high in the 1930s is strongly supported by the behaviour of the two wage series in both countries.[7] It thus appears that the $W/M$ curve in Chart 5.1 was abnormally high during the 1930s because the $W$ curve was abnormally high during that decade, and that Canadian money labour costs per unit of manufactured output of something like 5 or 6 per cent above the corresponding American figure represent the "normal" situation for the period under review.

Do excess costs of 5 or 6 per cent imply protected production, or does this figure simply represent an average level of transport costs for the imported goods? We have direct evidence, for the latter part of our period, that the excess of Canadian over American prices of manufactured goods reflected a heavy burden of protectionism. In 1954, when our $M/W$ figure stood at 107 per cent, Young's estimate of the cash cost of the Canadian tariff that year worked out to between $40 and $50 per capita, an estimate which for various reasons its author considered to be downward-biased.[8] Thus even when we discount the position of the $W/M$ curve in the 1930s to allow for the abnormally high $W$ curve in that period,

[7]From the figures provided in the statistical appendix to chapter 6 the reader may satisfy himself that in the United States the residual wage series maintained a clear differential above manufacturing wages throughout our period, that in Canada the same differential prevailed from 1927 to 1930, and from 1946 to 1955; and that during the 1930s there was virtually no differential between the residual and the manufacturing wage series in Canada. The residual wage series for Canada is a rough estimate; however, it behaves much like the two American series during the 1930s, while the Canadian manufacturing wage series falls much less than any of the other three series from 1929 to 1933.

[8]See J. H. Young, *Canadian Commercial Policy* (Ottawa, 1957), pp. 72–3, and Appendix A. The estimate is of course net of transport costs (p. 166). The chief upward bias in the estimate is the inclusion of producers' surplus resulting from the tariff; however, I share the author's opinion that on

Chart 5.1 clearly suggests that Canadian manufacturing has been protected, even heavily protected, throughout the period covered by our statistics.

## 2. TRENDS IN THE DATA

When the price systems of two economies are firmly linked to one another through international transactions a time series of relative wages in the two countries (the $W$ series) should move *in the same direction* as a time series of relative labour productivities in the two countries (the $M$ series), provided that no new distortion that affects the two countries differentially develops during the period being considered. In brief, in a situation of "moving equilibrium," with no change in differential distortions, wages in one country will be unable to advance relative to wages in the other unless labour productivity in the former is growing relative to labour productivity in the latter. These theoretical expectations are satisfactorily met in Chart 5.2 where the $M$ and $W$ curves, except for a few individual years, follow very similar trends.[9] In Chart 5.1 it is quite otherwise, especially during the pre-war period; the $W$ curve rises while the $M$ curve falls from 1927 to 1933, and from 1933 to 1939 precisely the reverse trends occur. In the post-war period a generally rising $W$ curve is matched with a generally falling $M$ curve.

The implication of this analysis is that the figures in Chart 5.1, particularly during the 1930s, were subject to the effects of a distortion that $(a)$ changed over time, $(b)$ affected Canada and the United States differentially, and $(c)$ was not apparent in the figures of Chart 5.2.

---

balance the estimate is likely to be downward-biased. Producers' surplus will be smaller the "flatter" are cost curves and supply curves; it is a fair presumption that in many, perhaps most, manufacturing industries the curves *are* fairly "flat." The estimate, it may be noted, if expressed on a per family basis, would amount to over 5 per cent of the annual wage figure for manufacturing in 1954.

[9] Year-to-year consistency in the figures should not be expected; adjustments between productivity and wages will be subject to frictions and lags, and for short periods changes in productivity will probably be reflected in profit margins rather than in wages. Our statements, then, refer to the general *trends* displayed by the series over subperiods of several years' duration.

Changes in protection in one of our countries relative to the other would be consistent with precisely this sort of distortion. When relative protection *changes* the two economies become temporarily "disconnected" and are free to go their separate ways until a new international equilibrium is established. Many of the pronounced movements of the curves in Chart 5.1 are consistent with what we know of the history of Canadian protectionism during this period. We cannot explain the gap that, according to our figures, was opened between the *M* and *W* curves in 1928, but the widening of the gap thereafter corresponds with the period of increasing protection in Canada that ran its course from the moderate tariff increase of 1929 to the Imperial Preference arrangements of 1932.[10] Whatever the effect of the Hawley-Smoot tariff in the United States (and it was probably a species of economic overkill) it was obviously less distorting to the American economy than the Canadian measures were to the Canadian economy, for Canadian earnings in manufacturing *rose* relative to American earnings from 1928 to 1933, at the same time as Canadian productivity *fell* relative to American productivity.

The absurd positions of the *M* and *W* curves in Chart 5.1 by 1933 suggest a free-floating Canadian manufacturing economy that has temporarily escaped the discipline of the international economy. (The behaviour and relative positions of the same curves in Chart 5.2 provide a striking contrast.) The descent to reality after 1934 was no doubt hastened by the much freer trading arrangements of 1935 between Canada and the United States, but the relative positions of the curves in 1939 suggest that the Canadian manufacturing sector was still out of balance with the international economy at the outbreak of the Second World War. The sharp fall in the *W* curve during the war period completed the adjustment. (Were Canadian wage controls inherently more effective than American controls? Or were they more effective because there was more economic reason for them to be effective?) The adjustment,

[10]See W. A. Mackintosh, *The Economic Background of Dominion-Provincial Relations* (Ottawa, 1949), pp. 89–96. Some of the individual tariff changes in the late 1920s may have involved increased protection. See pp. 52 and 84.

indeed, seems to have overshot the mark; the $W$ curve emerged from the war below the $M$ curve, but rose rapidly to approximately the same level in 1949, and by 1952 $W$ again exceeded $M$ by a sizable margin.

After 1949 the $M$ and $W$ curves in Chart 5.1 display a much closer relationship, both as to level and as to trend, than they did in the 1930s. Their new relationship is also consistent with the protection hypothesis. With no sharp change in protectionism during the postwar period something like an equilibrium relationship between the $M$ and $W$ curves was re-established. It should be noted, too, that the upward drift of the $W/M$ curve after 1948 was matched by a downward drift of the relative output curve—quite the opposite of the trends from 1928 to 1932 when rising relative costs in Canada were accompanied by *rising* relative outputs.[11] Thus during the "great postwar boom" in Canada manufacturing output, unsuccoured by increases in protection, grew slightly *less* rapidly than American manufacturing output. During the same period "residual" output grew considerably more rapidly in Canada than in the United States.

3. WAGES AND PROTECTED PRODUCTION

Tariff theory has very little to say about the effects of protection on *money* prices of the factors of production. Models are normally designed so that falling *real* wages result from unchanged money wages and increased product prices. In a dynamic context, however, there seems no reason why real wages should not be reduced below what they otherwise would have been by some combination of the rate of growth in money wages and the rate of growth in product prices; or, more generally, why protection and money wages should not be functionally related. It is interesting to study Chart 5.1 with this possibility in mind. During the "disequilibrium" period of the early 1930s, when protection was increasing in Canada,

[11]We should expect Canadian output to *fall* relative to American output when Canadian costs *rise* relative to American costs. Our $O$ and $W/M$ curves should therefore move in opposite directions. Manufacturing again fails the test in the 1930s; rising relative costs are associated with rising relative output from 1927 to 1932 and falling relative costs with falling relative output from 1933 to 1939.

105

the short-run effect seems to have been to raise relative Canadian wages in manufacturing (actually, to prevent them from falling as far as American wages, or as far as wages in the residual sector in Canada).[12] This "disequilibrium" relationship between protection and money wages is not inconsistent with the opposite relationship suggested by a comparison of two "equilibrium" periods in Chart 5.1. Thus inspection of the $W/M$ curve in Chart 5.1 suggests that money costs (prices) of manufactured goods in Canada and the United States bore about the same relationship to one another in 1926 and 1927 as they did in the early 1950s, both quiescent, "equilibrium" periods from the standpoint of tariff history, but that the relative Canadian : American wage series was definitely lower in the 1950s than it had been a quarter of a century earlier. If the reduction in relative money wages (actually the slower growth in money wages in Canada) between these two "equilibrium" periods is in fact related to protection, the burden of protection must have increased between the two periods.

The relative productivity curves in the charts indicate such an increase. The $M$ curve in Chart 5.1 shows that Canadian productivity relative to American productivity in manufacturing in the postwar period was slightly *lower* than, and gently *falling* relative to, its average level in the late 1920s and the 1930s. In the residual sector (Chart 5.2) relative Canadian productivity was definitely *rising* in the 1950s, and stood at an average level well above that of the 1930s and above the one observation for 1929.[13] Taken together, these observations mean that Canada's comparative disadvantage in manufacturing relative to residual output increased from the prewar to the postwar period. The great postwar expansion in Canadian manufacturing (which the $O$ curve in Chart 5.1 shows to have been not quite so great as the postwar expansion in American manufacturing) therefore took place in the face of increasing comparative disadvantage. Accordingly the burden

[12]This statement assumes some immobility of labour between the two sectors in Canada, an assumption that is credible at a time of heavy unemployment throughout the economy.
[13]I have not attempted to explain the trends in Chart 5.2 in any detail; the residual sector is so heterogeneous that there is little point in doing so. I have used it merely as contrasting background for Chart 5.1.

106

of protectionism must have increased. And since the level of the $W/M$ curve in the late 1920s was about the same as its level in the 1950s, it appears that the increased burden took the form of relatively lower Canadian money wages, rather than of relatively higher Canadian money costs (prices).[14]

## III

Reflection shows that the question, "Has the protective tariff in Canada actually protected Canadian manufacturing?" is but a particular example of the historian's eternal struggle to separate reality from appearance. The importance of distinguishing between them in the present case is, I hope, suggested by the earlier *a priori* argument to the effect that the export of a wide range of manufactured goods from the United States is proof that the American tariff has not given much, if any, protection to American manufacturing. But the reverse proposition is not necessarily true, and to prove that protection exists is much more difficult than to prove that it does not. In this essay I have tried to support the proposition that the Canadian tariff has been effective, at least over the thirty-year period covered by the present study, and in all probability from its inception. From one point of view the argument depends on a backward extrapolation of Young's convincing demonstration that the tariff was highly effective in the single year, 1954. From another point of view the present study purports to provide independent support for the proposition that the Canadian tariff has been effective. But rigorous empirical "proof" of the proposition is out of the question; as has been seen, the lack of sufficient information has forced me to fall back on a major assumption about production costs which, while not unreasonable, is of uncertain validity. All I am entitled to claim, I suppose, is that the statistical analysis does not invalidate the hypothesis that the Canadian tariff has been protective in fact as well as in intent. But the hypothesis and the facts do fit together very well . . .

[14]Many of the propositions suggested in the last two paragraphs are supported by the conclusions of the deductive analysis presented in chapter 3.

# 6

## The Role of the Tariff in
## Canadian Development

Although the Canadian policy of tariff protection for manufacturing has been in continuous operation for more than
eighty years, our knowledge of how it has affected the development of the Canadian economy is still fragmentary. Before
laying out my own attack on the problem of the long-run
effects of protection in Canada, it will be well to review briefly
what has already been done by others.

  Canadian economic historians have always paid a good deal
of attention to tariff policy, but for the most part they have
assumed that protection has done only what it was intended
to do, namely, to expand manufacturing, and they have displayed little curiosity about its possible effects on non-protected
industries, growth rates, factor prices, factor supplies, and
other economic variables. There are, of course, exceptions.
The late Professor Fowke dealt with the effects of the tariff
on land rents and the domestic terms of trade between agriculture and manufacturing; Professor Mackintosh discussed
the possible effect of the tariff on population size; and Professor McDiarmid studied in considerable detail the effects of
tariff changes on prices, market share, output, and employment, in a few major Canadian industries.[1] In general though,

[1]V. C. Fowke, *The National Policy and The Wheat Economy* (Toronto,
1957); W. A. Mackintosh, *The Economic Background of Dominion-Provincial Relations*, Appendix 3 of the Royal Commission on Dominion-
Provincial Relations (Ottawa, 1939); O. J. McDiarmid, *Commercial
Policy in the Canadian Economy* (Cambridge, Mass., 1946).

Canadian economic historians have been content to deal with the tariff in terms of broad generalizations and to interpret it as an integral part of a "developmental strategy" aimed at nation-building. They have, in fact, been at pains to justify the Canadian euphemism for protection, the "National Policy," a term artfully exploited by Sir John A. Macdonald when he gave Canadians their first determinedly protectionist tariff in 1879. While insisting on a political interpretation of protection, Canadian economic historians have not disputed the trade theorist's proposition that a tariff lowers the standard of living in the country that imposes it. They have, therefore, become willing victims of the mercantilist contradiction that a nation can become richer by making its citizens poorer. In Canada this contradiction has been enshrined in a beautiful piece of word-magic that would surely have delighted Macdonald himself. The tariff, historians have taught us, is "the price of being a Canadian." In reality, of course, it is the price we pay for our protected manufacturing industry—very often the bribe we pay foreigners to establish manufacturing capacity in Canada.

Recent empirical studies of tariff problems by Canadian economists have been much more informative, if much less politically persuasive, than the historians' grandiloquent gloss on the National Policy. The old objection to a tariff structure as the mother of monopoly has been modernized by showing in detail how protection fosters inefficient, oligopolistic forms of market organization in Canada.[2] Estimates of the optimum technical size of plant have been compared with the size of the Canadian market to deflate the claim that the Canadian market is too small to permit Canadian manufacturers to reap "the economies of scale."[3] These studies should make it more difficult for politicians to use the hoary "infant industry"

[2]H. C. Eastman, "The Canadian Tariff and the Efficiency of the Canadian Economy," *Papers and Proceedings of the American Economic Association,* May, 1964, pp. 437–48; and two papers by H. C. Eastman and S. Stykolt: "A Model for the Study of Protected Oligopolies" in the *Economic Journal,* June, 1960, pp. 336–47; and "Le fonctionnement de deux oligopoles protégés au Canada" in *Economie Appliqué,* janvier–février, 1962, pp. 27–50.
[3]H. E. English, *Industrial Structure in Canada's International Competitive Position* (Canadian Trade Committee, 1964).

argument for protection. (Most propositions that derive from this argument are in any event based on the false assumption that it is a national market, rather than the world market, that is of relevance to entrepreneurs. If a plant is expected to be uneconomic at a scale of output sufficient to serve the domestic market but to be economic at a larger output, entrepreneurs should obviously plan to produce the larger output and export the surplus above the home market's requirements. Economists have been much too generous in admitting the logical respectability of the infant industry argument. Historians have long known that many major industries have, from their infancy, been based on export markets as well as the domestic market.) Finally, Professor Young's estimate of the cash cost of the Canadian tariff—a study made for the Gordon Commission, but, significantly, disavowed by that Commission—showed that Canadians paid close to a billion dollars (or over 4 per cent of GNP) for their protectionist policy in 1956.[4] In one year, in other words, Canadians subsidized their manufacturing industries by an amount approximately equal to *twice* the *capital* cost of the St. Lawrence Seaway. This shocking statistic has been greeted with impressive apathy by Canadian officialdom. As so often happens in a country where the "Establishment" lacks competition, unpalatable findings have been ignored without being refuted.

The present essay is an empirical study of Canadian economic growth under protectionism; it may be regarded, from one point of view, as an extensive analysis of the background of Professor Young's statistic, that is to say, as a study of several ways in which Canadian growth has been distorted by the National Policy. One of its main conclusions, curiously enough, is that Young's estimate of the cash cost of the Canadian tariff, interpreted as an estimate of the effect of the tariff in lowering Canadian GNP is wrong as to sign—I think the tariff has probably *increased* Canadian GNP!—and yet that the same statistic, interpreted as an estimate of the effect of the tariff in lowering Canadian GNP per capita, is probably much too low!

[4]J. H. Young, *Canadian Commercial Policy* (Ottawa, 1957), pp. 72–3 and Appendix A. See also chap. 5, n. 8, above.

110

# I

The method employed in the study is discussed at length in chapter 4. Here, only a few reminders of its specific features are necessary. Each of the numbers presented in Chart 6.1 is

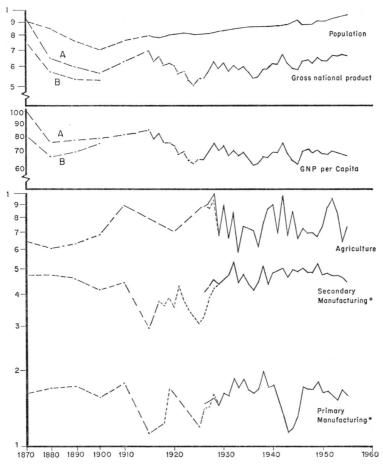

CHART 6.1. CANADIAN:AMERICAN PERCENTAGES: VARIOUS SERIES, 1870–1955
(All underlying value data in 1929 dollars)

Notes on Canadian data
Long dashes: Decennial data or estimates
: A. Firestone's estimates
: B. Hartland's estimates
Short dashes: Deflated value estimates
Solid lines: Official data or reliable estimates
*As percentages of total manufacturing in the United States.

111

a percentage fraction composed of a Canadian numerator and an American denominator. Canadian:American percentages are calculated for each year for six magnitudes (population, GNP, GNP per capita, and value added in three sectors) and the resulting "time series of percentages" are shown on the chart. The approximate *levels* of the series reflect mainly the difference in *size* of the two economies. I shall have relatively little to say about the levels of the series, however; my main interest is in their *trends*. An uptrend indicates that Canada has grown faster than the United States in respect to the magnitude measured by that series, and a downtrend, of course, indicates the reverse. As was noted in chapter 4, the general expectation, based on the large number of similarities between the two economies, is that the series should be trendless. When trends are observed, the explanation is to be sought in terms of one or another of the three main "differences" between the two economies—the protection difference, the resource difference, and the immigration difference—and it has already been argued that the main effect of the "resource" difference is to impart an uptrend to the series, except in the case of agricultural output. Taken together, the series provide an account of the relative experience of Canada and the United States in several important aspects of economic growth over an eighty-year period. My purpose is to examine the series individually and in relation to each other, to identify trends that contradict expected behaviour, and, as well as may be, to explain why the Canadian pattern of growth differs from the American. I shall work backwards in time, starting with the period 1926–55 when the statistical data are at their most reliable, and concluding with a few comments on the period from 1870 to 1925, when the Canadian data are scarce and based largely on rather rough estimates.

### 1. 1926–1955

(*a*) *Trends in Output.* Consider first the four "output" series: GNP, and the "value added" series for agriculture, secondary manufacturing, and primary manufacturing.[5] Agriculture is

[5]For definitions and statistical sources and procedures, see the Appendix to this chapter.

included partly because statistics for this sector were readily available, and partly because it remained a large sector of the Canadian economy throughout the interwar period. (From the late 1920s to the early 1950s agricultural output in Canada declined from 16 to slightly less than 8 per cent of GNP; in the United States the comparable figures were between 10 and 11 per cent for the earlier period and slightly over 6 per cent for the later period.) My chief interest lies in the manufacturing series. The Canadian figures are divided into the primary and secondary categories mainly to see whether the primary sector, which is for the most part unprotected, behaves differently from the secondary sector, much of which is heavily protected. Over our period secondary manufacturing rose from 20 to almost 24 per cent of Canadian GNP, and primary manufacturing from 7 to slightly over 8 per cent of GNP. The total figures, 27 and 32 per cent respectively, may be compared with the analogous American figures of 27.5 per cent for the late 1920s and 33.3 per cent for the early 1950s. The agriculture and manufacturing comparisons combined therefore include about 40 per cent of total output in each country; the other 60 per cent, covering all other economic sectors, is of course included in the GNP series.

For the period as a whole the GNP series displays a pronounced uptrend, the two manufacturing series a slight uptrend, and the agricultural series a moderate downtrend. Closer inspection, however, reveals that these over-all trends are the resultants of quite different trends in the prewar period (1926–39) and the postwar period (1946–55). In the prewar period the GNP and agriculture series trended downward, especially after 1928; primary manufacturing showed a consistent upward trend; and secondary manufacturing moved upward until 1934 and then sagged slightly. I shall ignore the disturbed war period for the most part. Its main effect seems to have been to shift the level of our series up a notch, except for primary manufacturing; in particular, secondary manufacturing in Canada grew more rapidly than manufacturing in the United States during the war years. In the postwar period the prewar trends were all reversed. The GNP series moved sharply upward; the agricultural series fluctuated wildly, but showed

113

an uptrend on balance; primary manufacturing and secondary manufacturing trended slowly but definitely downward.

Since the trend in secondary manufacturing opposed the movement in the GNP series in both the prewar and postwar periods, it is clear that trends in Canadian manufacturing do not determine the over-all behaviour of the Canadian economy relative to the American economy. The data in Chart 6.1 cast serious doubt on the common assumption in Canada that the country's potential for growth lies mainly in secondary manufacturing, especially in what has recently been dignified by the term "sophisticated" manufacturing. Although on balance secondary manufacturing in Canada grew slightly more than manufacturing in the United States during the thirty-year period under consideration, its relative growth was confined mainly to two periods: the years 1926 to 1934, and the war years. The bulk of the first period was characterized by increasing protection in Canada and by depression, and the increased protection seems to have prevented manufacturing output from falling quite so far in Canada as it did in the United States. Nevertheless, Canadian manufacturing output fell to low levels; despite increased protection the performance of the manufacturing sector failed to dispel the depression, and indeed aggravated it in several respects. The second period of relative growth in secondary manufacturing occurred during the war years, and is probably to be explained by the *de facto* increase in protection afforded by wartime conditions. During the two periods of "normal" prosperity covered by our series—the recovery from the depths of the depression in the last half of the 1930s, and the decade of prosperity after the Second World War—secondary manufacturing in Canada grew slightly less rapidly than manufacturing in the United States. The contrasts between the trends of primary and secondary manufacturing, as shown in the chart, are not pronounced, but are perhaps significant. Although unprotected, primary manufacturing suffered no more than secondary manufacturing during the early depression years, recovered more rapidly in the later thirties, and performed as well as secondary manufacturing in the postwar period.

114

Since the trends in the GNP series in Chart 6.1 cannot be explained by the manufacturing series, they must be explained by developments in other parts of the economy. The downtrend in the GNP series in the prewar period may be explained in part by the downtrend in the agriculture series, for agriculture was at that time still a statistically significant part of the Canadian economy; in part it must be explained by downtrends in sectors of the economy that are not identified in the chart. The sharp uptrend in the GNP series after 1946 is quite surprising in view of the downtrend in secondary manufacturing and the small weight that must be attached to the uptrend in the agriculture series. Relative Canadian:American output in the unidentified sectors must have grown even more rapidly than the growth in Canadian GNP relative to American GNP. However, it must be remembered that the GNP series includes growth arising from the statistical "shift effect" that results when resources in an economy are moved from low (as measured) income sectors to high (as measured) income sectors. This effect has been much more pronounced in Canada than in the United States during the postwar period; the flight from the farm, which had been underway in the United States throughout the interwar period, became important in Canada only during the Second World War and proceeded more rapidly in Canada than in the United States during the postwar decade.[6] Nevertheless it is probably true that most of the increase in Canadian GNP relative to American GNP has

[6]See A. Maddison, "Productivity in an Expanding Economy," *Economic Journal*, September, 1952, pp. 584–94. The author estimates that the increase in over-all productivity in Canada due to shifts in employment between eight sectors was 7.71 per cent from 1931 to 1949 (as compared with a roughly similar estimate of 4.6 per cent for the United States for the same period) and 6.48 per cent from 1941 to 1949. These figures are to be compared with an increase of "productivity proper" (output per man not attributable to shifts) of 64 per cent from 1931 to 1949 and only 17 per cent between 1941 and 1949. "The importance of structural change is much greater in the later half of the period than in the earlier half." (p. 589) The author notes that productivity in manufacturing "grew more slowly than in the rest of the economy" (p. 590) and attributes a significant part of the growth in over-all productivity in Canada during this period to a higher level of general economic activity and thus a better utilization of social capital, economies of scale, and forced growth during the war (pp. 591–93). G. D. Sutton, "Productivity in Canada," *Canadian*

resulted from a more rapid growth of Canadian output in non-agricultural, non-manufacturing sectors, particularly in such resource industries as mining and forestry—productivity increases in these industries in Canada were much greater than in Canadian manufacturing during the postwar period— and in population-sensitive sectors such as construction, trade, and public utilities, for a glance at the chart shows that the Canadian population grew much more rapidly than the American in the postwar decade.

(b) *Trends in the Population, GNP, and GNP per Capita Series.* The almost continuous rise in the population series throughout the whole period from 1926 to 1955, and its somewhat sharper rise after 1946, produced, in conjunction with the GNP series, a declining trend in the GNP per capita series in both the prewar and postwar periods. This latter series moved upward, on balance, during the war period, but for the whole thirty-year period its trend was at best zero, and perhaps slightly downwards. Here, then, is a major mystery; over a thirty-year period Canada has grown relative to the United States in terms of population and GNP, but relative to the United States it has grown not one whit—perhaps it has even shrunk slightly—in terms of GNP per capita. Why?[7]

---

*Journal of Economics and Political Science,* May, 1953, pp. 185–201, states that, "The shift of labour from farm to non-farm employment has in itself accounted for about a third of the rise in over-all output per man-year since 1950" (p. 195), and notes that since the thirties this shift "has resulted in production per man increasing more rapidly for the economy as a whole than for either of the component parts [farm and non-farm]" (p. 195). See also, J. Alterman's note on "The Estimation of Real Domestic Product . . . in Canada" by V. R. Berlinguette and F. H. Leacy in *Output, Input and Productivity Measurement* (NBER Studies in Income and Wealth, vol. XXV), p. 249, where the author calculates that the shift from agricultural to non-agricultural employment from 1947 to 1955 accounted for about 15 per cent of the increase in over-all productivity in Canada, as compared with 8 per cent in the United States.

[7]One possible answer, developed from the standpoint of economic theory, has already been given. Throughout the analysis in chapter 3 we stressed the conclusion that the effect of a constant tariff is to create a divergence between the GNP and GNP per capita growth rates. The United States denominators in Chart 6.1 serve to represent the "control" situation imagined in chapter 3, and the divergence between the GNP and GNP per capita series in Chart 6.1 therefore conforms to the theoretical expectation derived in chapter 3.

The rate of natural increase in population has been about 25 per cent higher in Canada than in the United States, but the fact that native Canadians are free to emigrate to the United States and have done so in large numbers for a century or more renders untenable any simple hypothesis that "population pressure" explains the secular growth in the Canadian population relative to the American population. Moreover immigration, emigration, and net migration have played a much larger role in Canadian population changes than in American population changes during the past forty years. Table 6.1 gives some idea of the vast flux of people across Canada's borders, and of the abrupt changes in both the absolute and percentage effects of migration on the Canadian

TABLE 6.1

Canadian Population Experience*
(millions of people)

| Period | Population increase | Natural increase | Net migration | Gross immigration | Gross emigration |
|---|---|---|---|---|---|
| 1921–31 | 1.59 | 1.36 | .23 | 1.20 | .97 |
| 1931–41 | 1.13 | 1.22 | —.09 | .15 | .24 |
| 1941–51 | 2.14 | 1.97 | .17 | .55 | .38 |
| 1951–56 | 2.07 | 1.47 | .60 | .78 | .18 |

*The figures for population increase are taken from M. C. Urquhart and K. A. H. Buckley, eds., *Historical Statistics of Canada* (Toronto, 1965), Series A-2. Immigration and emigration figures are from the same volume, Series B102 and B103. The population increase for 1941–51 excludes Newfoundland.

population. It is in the volatile figures of Canadian emigration and immigration that much of the explanation of changes in the relative growth rate of Canadian and American population must be sought.[8]

The large and persistent differential between the Canadian

[8]In an unpublished paper D. J. Daly has shown that throughout most of the period since 1870 gross immigration has been much larger as a proportion of the Canadian population than of the American population; and that as between the two countries relative changes in net migration have been much more important than relative changes in natural increase in determining relative changes in total population. ("Kuznets Cycles in Canada," paper presented to the Ottawa Chapter, Canadian Political Science Association, March 13, 1962, p. 8, and Charts 2 and 3.)

and American standards of living constitutes a standing incentive for Canadians to emigrate to the United States. But while the *direction* of international migration is determined largely by international differences in the standard of living, the volume and timing of such migration is probably dependent mainly on international differences in the level of "job opportunities," and especially on the state of the labour market in the country of intended destination. During the 1930s, when the unemployment rate was even higher in the United States than it was in Canada, emigration from Canada dropped to low levels, though gross emigration was about 20 per cent of the natural increase, and net emigration about 7 per cent of the natural increase. Since net migration was probably close to zero in the United States during the decade, the Canadian population grew relative to the American at a rate slightly less than the difference in the crude rates of natural increase would imply.

It was quite otherwise in the prosperous postwar period. Emigration from Canada to the United States rose throughout the period but, since prosperity reigned in both countries, the movement was small by historical standards. Immigration into Canada, however, approached record levels and in proportion to population was seven times larger than immigration into the United States. Even though per capita incomes in Canada were 30 per cent below those in the United States they were higher than incomes in Europe; and, since American quotas severely restricted immigration from Europe, Canada did not lack for immigrants. The net result was that Canadian population rose relative to American population by perhaps a third more than the difference in the crude rates of natural increase would have implied.

Though changes in net migration play a much larger role in population change in Canada than in the United States, the fact remains that Canadian population grows relative to American population both in season and out. The relative standard of living in the two countries, on the other hand, has remained virtually unchanged, on average, for at least forty years. And since unemployment rates in the two countries have not differed greatly over the long run, Canadian GNP has grown faster than American GNP by about the same margin as Canadian population has grown relative to American population. The major question therefore still remains: Why is an equal percentage increase in the standard of living in Canada and the United States accompanied by a percentage increase in both population and GNP in Canada significantly larger than that in the United States? To phrase the problem in a slightly different way, consider a prolonged period of prosperity (for example, the postwar decade) during which the standard of living in both countries rises by roughly the same percentage. The question is then why the boom in Canada creates more job opportunities than can be filled by the natural increase in population, and therefore results in net immigration, while in the United States the boom is "staffed" by a much smaller percentage increase in population. Why is Canadian growth "population-biased"? There are no sure answers to these questions, but some suggestions may be made.

In the United States, whenever technological progress and the natural increase of population create more job opportunities than can be filled by the natural increase in the labour force, the excess demand for labour will be extinguished primarily by a rise in wages because American laws strictly limit the possibility of extinguishing it by an increase in immigration.[9] In Canada an excess demand for labour is likely to be a much more common feature of economic development than it is in the United States. In the first place the Canadian tariff, by exerting a continuous downward pressure on the Canadian standard of living, leads to continuous emigration from Canada and thus a continuous depletion of the natural increase in the Canadian labour force. Given Canadian immigration policy, this deficit tends to be made good by immigration; emigrants from the labour force thus tend to be replaced by immigrants to the labour force at the same money wage. This part of the mechanism of adjustment to an excess demand for labour in

[9]The increase in the female labour force, which has been proceeding more rapidly in the United States than in Canada, is a form of "immigration" that raises the per capita income of a *given* population. But see the following footnote.

Canada has little or no effect on the relation between GNP or GNP per capita in the two countries; there is nothing in the offsetting emigration and immigration to change Canadian GNP or GNP per capita, and little to change the relationship of the Canadian figures to their American counterparts. (A given emigration from Canada to the United States, of course, has only about one-tenth the percentage effect on the American labour force that it has on the Canadian labour force.)

A second reason why situations of an excess demand for labour are likely to be more common in Canada than in the United States is implicit in arguments that have already been presented. Thus it was argued in chapter 4 that during this century technology has been differentially favourable to Canada relative to the United States, and in chapter 3 that the Canadian tariff tends to translate differentially favourable improvements in productivity into a larger supply of job opportunities than the same relative improvement would have created in the absence of the tariff. Given Canadian immigration policy, *this* sort of excess demand for labour also tends to be satisfied by immigration at existing wage rates rather than by an increase in Canadian wages relative to American wages. In this case, Canadian GNP grows relative to American GNP (by the amount of the immigration to the labour force times the going wage), but Canadian GNP per capita remains unchanged. This part of the mechanism of adjustment to an excess demand for labour in Canada, therefore, could explain both the uptrend in the GNP series and the stability of the GNP per capita series that we observe in Chart 6.1.

The question now arises as to why any excess demand for labour in Canada that arises from the interaction of the Canadian tariff and differentially favourable technological trends should be satisfied by immigration rather than by a differentially large increase in wages in Canada. The answer seems to be: "an unwitting conspiracy" by business, labour, and government. If differentially favourable technological trends reduce Canadian costs of production relative to American costs of production in most industries, management in these industries will be able to "afford" to reduce the Canadian-

American wage differential. However, they would probably prefer, if possible, to enhance their status by increasing output on the basis of immigrant labour at the going wage rate (and selling the additional output to the additional population) rather than to increase their wage-bill at the existing output. And of course there will be some protected firms whose costs have not decreased relative to American costs, and they would be forced out of business by a wage increase; since their prices are pegged at a ceiling set by the American price plus the tariff, they could not pass on the wage increase by a price increase. On the whole, therefore, business probably prefers an increase in immigration to an increase in wages.

Labour says that it would prefer a wage increase to an increase in immigration. But let us see. First of all, the unions in those firms that would be forced out of business if the Canadian:American wage gap were narrowed may well reconsider their position, and agree to go along with management's view of the situation. Moreover, labour generally will probably find it very easy to get the same percentage wage increases in Canada that have been achieved in the United States—after all, both business and government would frown on an increase in the Canadian:American wage differential, for that would involve an increased loss of Canadian labour to the United States—but very difficult to get anything more, because a narrowing of the Canadian:American wage gap would amount to a reduction of Canadian protection and the forcing of some Canadian firms to the wall. On the whole, there is much to be said for a quiet life.

Government's role in the mechanism seems to reflect an interest in a Big Canada—a willingness, up to a certain point, to increase Canada's population even if that involves a lower standard of living for Canadians than would otherwise be possible. In any event, Government's *willingness* to solve the recurring problem of an excess demand for labour in Canada by promoting immigration whenever the economy can "absorb" more people at the going wage rate, rather than by allowing nature to take its course (which would involve an increase in wages and a reduction of the Canadian-American income gap), clearly fits in with the main preconception of business, rather than labour, as to the proper cure for "wage inflation."

But the old economic ways may be changing in Canada. As I write, two major unions—the automobile workers and the steel workers—are pressing for wage parity between Canada and the United States. If the movement for wage parity spreads there is some hope that the Canadian:American income gap will narrow in the future. A relative rise in Canadian wages would of course mean a *de facto* reduction in present levels of protection, and a consequent reduction in the size of the protected sector. The required adjustments in the economy would be substantial, but if they are spread over several years —as they undoubtedly would be—they should cause no disruption.

In the last several paragraphs we have sketched out in rather "intuitive" terms a model of how protection affects the Canadian economy over time—a model that was developed in more technical terms in chapters 2 and 3. A movement to wage parity would reduce protection and simply shift the model into reverse gear. As parity spread and wages rose the excess demand for labour would be reduced; immigration would be reduced, both because of the smaller excess demand for labour and because the "replacement" demand for immigration would fall as emigration to the United States fell; population and GNP would rise more slowly than they otherwise would have, but GNP per capita would rise more rapidly. At the end of the transition period a new equilibrium would be established in which the Canadian population would be smaller but richer than it would have been if parity had not been achieved; in which gross emigration would be smaller and gross immigration smaller still; and in which the relative size of the protected sector, and thus the per capita burden of protection, had been reduced. After labour had relieved Canadians of part of their protectionist burden by achieving wage parity, it would be up to the government to finish the job by phasing out the tariff.

(c) *The Level of the GNP per Capita Series.* Can Canadian protection explain the 25 to 30 per cent gap that has persisted for so long between per capita income in Canada and the United States? Let me say to begin with that I do not believe that the "geographical" and "resource" differences between Canada and the United States can explain the whole difference between the Canadian and American standards of living. A significant fraction of this difference, in my judgment, must be due to a man-made difference, or, in brief, must reflect economic policy in Canada that is inferior to that in the United States.

The reasons for part of the income difference are obvious. The labour force participation rate is lower in Canada than in the United States; when this difference was "allowed for" in a rough arithmetical analysis of the income difference in the two countries for 1955, the 30 per cent difference in income per capita was reduced to a 20 per cent difference per member of the labour force, i.e., a little over $1,200. It must be noted, though, that the lower labour force participation rate in Canada is in part a *result* of the income differential; leisure in Canada is much cheaper than in the United States.[10] The figure of 20 per cent is therefore probably biased downward. A generous adjustment of $125 per member of the entire labour force was then made for the larger share of the Canadian labour force in agriculture, a "low-income" industry, and the Canadian:American income differential was thereby reduced to $1075—a little over 18 per cent. Twice this adjustment, or $250 per member of the labour force, was

[10]In its *Second Annual Review* (Ottawa, 1966) the Economic Council of Canada italicized its finding that the income gap per person employed was less than 20 per cent (p. 58). But this is mere arithmetic, and makes no allowance for the probable functional relationship noted in the text. A similar argument applies to the educational qualifications of the labour force; but here the Council *does* note that the deficiency of the Canadian labour force in this respect is partly due to the fact that in the United States "significantly higher average incomes [accrue] to those with higher education." (p. 58) In typically Canadian fashion the Council recommends that the deficiency be righted by an increased supply of educational services rather than by increased wages for skill and thus an increased demand for educational services. The assumption seems to be that those receiving higher education in Canada will stay in Canada at lower wages than they can earn in the United States, an assumption that is theoretically improbable and historically incorrect.

then made for the possibility that the pattern of all other industries is biased toward "low-income" industries as compared with the pattern in the United States; this further subtraction of $250 reduced the "adjusted income per worker" differential to 14 per cent of the American figure. Finally, an allowance of $300 per member of the Canadian labour force, or about 5 per cent of the income per member of the American labour force, was made for "geographical and other" disabilities of the Canadian economy; this reduced the "unexplained" Canadian:American differential in income per member of the labour force to $525, or 8.7 per cent of the American figure. Let us call the unexplained difference 8 per cent.

An 8 per cent difference in income per worker is enormous. Professor Fogel has calculated that the advent of railways in the United States increased per capita income by something less than 2 per cent. The calculation was based on agricultural traffic only; to allow for manufactured freight and passenger traffic, triple this figure and make it 6.[11] On a very rough and generous guess Denison calculates that "the total cost of conditions that lead to misallocation or prevent efficient use of resources and that could, in principle, be removed" amounts to between 6 and 7 per cent of American incomes in recent decades.[12] Whatever institutional factor accounts for the "unexplained" difference of 8 per cent in per worker incomes in Canada and the United States, is therefore a very large and significant force; it reduces Canadian incomes by considerably more than the amount that railroads increased incomes in the United States, and by considerably more than all economic inefficiencies in the United States reduced American income in the 1950s.

Professor Young's calculation of the cash cost of the Canadian tariff suggested that protection reduced Canadian GNP by about one billion dollars in 1956, or the equivalent of

[11]R. W. Fogel, "Railroads as an Analogy to the Space Effort," *Economic Journal*, March, 1966, p. 40.
[12]E. F. Denison, *The Sources of Economic Growth in the United States*, Supplementary Paper no. 13, Committee for Economic Development (Washington, 1962), p. 199.

almost $180 per member of the labour force; this amounts to over one-third of our "unexplained" difference of $525 in Canadian and American income per worker. Yet it can be argued that Professor Young's estimate of the "per worker" burden of the Canadian tariff is much too low. A "cash-cost" estimate of the burden of protection measures only the increase in the prices of *goods* attributable to the tariff. But as was argued in chapter 3, and again in chapter 5, the tariff may also reduce money *incomes*, and this possibility alone might lead one to increase considerably Professor Young's estimate of the burden of the Canadian tariff. Moreover, as the late Professor Salter argued in *Productivity and Technical Change*, low wages cheapen labour and delay the date at which the most modern machine methods of production are adopted; thus to the extent that the most modern machine methods make for the lowest costs of production, the tariff, by cheapening labour, tends to perpetuate high-cost production and keep the productivity of labour lower than it otherwise would be. In addition, high-cost manufactured goods become inputs into unprotected industries and therefore tend to raise costs throughout the economy. None of these social costs of the tariff gets included in a "cash cost" estimate of the burden of protection.

It is not unreasonable, I submit, to suppose that on a true reckoning of *all* the costs of protectionism, the Canadian tariff would explain most of the "unexplained residual" of at least 8 per cent in the Canadian-American income differential. And, as was suggested above, the low level of Canadian incomes relative to American incomes itself tends to perpetuate many inefficiencies in the Canadian economy. The thesis, then, is that the Canadian tariff explains a large part of the Canadian-American income differential.

## 2. 1870–1925

The data for this period, especially the Canadian data, are neither numerous enough nor reliable enough to provide a basis for fine analysis. But even if there were no data limitations, a comparative analysis of this period would be of doubtful utility because the Canadian:American comparison in the period 1870 to 1925 is much less "fair" and "meaningful" than it is in the period after 1925. The reason is that neither economy had reached its present geographical extent in 1870. New resources were still being "found"—for example, Pittsburgh coal and Mesabi iron in the United States—and new areas still being occupied—the American Midwest after 1870, the Canadian West after 1900. The "discovery" of new resources and the occupation of new areas occurred at different times in the two economies, and the difference in timing itself dominates the trends in the series of Chart 6.1, particularly during the nineteenth century and the first decade of the twentieth. In general, then, we cannot squeeze much, if any, new knowledge out of the Canadian:American percentages for these years. Nevertheless the data have descriptive value; they serve both to confirm the validity of general historical interpretations of the period, and to illustrate, over a longer period of time, some parts of the analysis based on the post-1925 period.

The dramatic decline in most of our series from 1870 to 1900 is consistent with the main tenor of historical writings on this period. The post-Civil War boom in the United States was perhaps the longest and strongest surge of economic growth that has ever been experienced in any country. Canada's growth in absolute terms was quite respectable; in primary manufacturing Canadian growth almost matched the American experience, and, if we are to believe the figures, agricultural output in Canada grew fully as fast as agricultural output in the United States. Over-all, however, Canada could not begin to match the American performance and the decline of the population and GNP series is not in the least surprising.

The GNP per capita series, especially when Firestone's figures are used, suggests that the differential between Canadian and American incomes from 1870 to 1910 was considerably smaller than it has been during the past forty years. An anti-protectionist would like to be able to associate the sharp drop in the series from 1870 to 1880 with the inauguration of protection in Canada, but since the National Policy was only introduced in 1879 it could hardly have had much effect on the figures for 1880! The drop is almost certainly due to the extremely rapid growth in the United States during the 1870s. It is interesting to note the effectiveness of emigration from 1870 to 1900 as a mechanism whereby Canadian per capita incomes were kept in step with those in the United States even when GNP in the United States was growing much more rapidly than in Canada. Net emigration from Canada occurred during each of the last three decades of the century, and after the initial widening of the Canadian:American income differential from 1870 to 1880 emigration was large enough to prevent any further relative decline in the Canadian standard of living; Hartland's figures suggest, indeed, that the differential narrowed considerably during the last twenty years of the century, i.e., that Canadian GNP per capita was rising more rapidly than the American, even though Canadian GNP was growing less rapidly.

The inauguration of the National Policy in Canada in 1879 left little imprint on the series in Chart 6.1, partly because trends in the aggregative series, as noted above, were dominated by other factors, and partly because secondary manufacturing was in any event a small part of the Canadian economy in the nineteenth century. Value added in secondary manufacturing rose from about 12 per cent of GNP in 1870 to about 16 per cent in 1900, but only surpassed value added in agriculture sometime between 1910 and 1920 (probably during the First World War). Nor are the manufacturing figures themselves very informative. However, it may be calculated from the figures presented in the Appendix to this chapter that between 1870 and 1900 the output of secondary manufacturing in Canada increased by 230 per cent of the 1870 figure while manufacturing in the United States increased by about 275 per cent. The Canadian performance seems suspiciously good in view of the fact that the American market was growing by leaps and bounds during these years while the Canadian market was growing very much more slowly, and in view of the fact that technological trends were running strongly in favour of American industry during the age of steel and coal.

The uptrend in all the series of Chart 6.1 from 1900 to

1910 is, like the downtrends of the previous thirty years, consistent with the conventional historical wisdom. The American economy continued to grow very rapidly during the decade, but it was outpaced by the Canadian economy which during these years experienced the greatest boom in its history to date. Even the standard of living rose faster in Canada than in the United States! Relative Canadian growth was slightest in secondary manufacturing.[13] The hallmarks of the boom were the opening of the Canadian West, associated constructional activity, and rapid expansion in mining, pulp and paper, and hydro-electric projects. The last three items suggest that the trend of technology had begun to tilt in Canada's favour.

It is difficult to make much sense out of the data between 1910 and 1925. The trends may be distorted because the great Canadian boom probably reached its peak in 1912 or 1913, years for which we have no observations, and because the observations for 1915 reflect the year of maximum wartime disorganization in the Canadian economy. The levels of the series may also be incorrect since the Canadian figures before 1926 are distinctly inferior in quality to those from 1926 on; in particular, the annual manufacturing figures for Canada from 1917 to 1925 inclusive are simply deflated value series. About all that is clear from Chart 6.1 is that most of the economic gains that Canada had made relative to the United States during the first dozen years of the century were lost during the next dozen years. Only agriculture, perhaps, maintained its position relative to American growth; the manufacturing series slipped badly at the outbreak of the War and again at the end of the War. Even the population series dipped after 1915, a reflection of the sharp reduction of European immigration to Canada during the war period, and again from 1922 to 1926. On balance the Canadian population grew as fast as the American, but Canadian GNP grew

[13]Canadian manufacturing output during this period probably also benefitted from a shift of production from the home to the factory, a shift which had been substantially completed in the United States by 1900. For a delightful literary discussion of shifts see G. A. Elliott, "The Impersonal Market," in *Canadian Journal of Economics and Political Science*, November, 1958, pp. 453–64, esp. 461–2.

much more slowly. The result was a rapid widening in the Canadian:American income differential; GNP per capita in Canada apparently fell from about 80 per cent of the American figure around 1915 to less than 70 per cent of the American figure in the middle 1920s. During the four years 1926 to 1929, American figures show that an average of 80,000 Canadians a year arrived in the United States—this during a period when the Canadian economy was reasonably prosperous, and again, for a few years, growing faster than the United States. On balance, the Canadian economy seems to have turned in a disappointing performance in the fifteen years from 1910 to 1925. The explanation remains a mystery, but protection must account for part of the relative decline in the Canadian standard of living. The share of secondary manufacturing in Canadian GNP had risen from 14 per cent in 1880 to 16 per cent in 1900 and 20 per cent in 1926, and as the protected sector became a larger part of the whole the individual's burden of protection grew; the National Policy was becoming more expensive.

## II

Finally, by way of summary, consider a few comments relating to the whole period covered by the Chart. If we use Firestone's figures for the nineteenth century, and compare the levels of our series for, say, some visual average of 1870 and 1880 on the one hand and the early 1950s on the other, we would conclude that Canadian output has grown no faster than American output over an eighty-year period; only the agricultural series showed any net gain, and by the 1950s agriculture was a small and declining part of GNP. What is striking is that the population series stood considerably higher at the end of the period, and that, accordingly, the GNP per capita series was considerably lower in the 1950s than the 1870s. The Hartland figures for GNP would show the same things if the comparison were based on the 1870 figure alone; if based on the 1880 figure alone, the relative growth in

Canadian GNP would have been virtually the same as relative growth in Canadian population, and the Canadian-American income differential would therefore be judged to be about the same in 1955 as it was in 1880. However, this eighty-year comparison is probably almost meaningless since we know that the net outcome for the whole period was the result of very different trends as between the nineteenth and twentieth centuries. A comparison of trends after 1900 is much more illuminating.

Since 1900 the "population-bias" of Canadian growth shows up clearly. The population series trends upward almost continuously. The GNP series rises on balance, but irregularly, and a little less than the population series. The net result was that the Canadian-American income differential seems to have been slightly wider at mid-century than it was in 1900.[14]

The relative growth in Canadian GNP after 1900 was mostly in the non-manufacturing sectors of the economy. The modest relative gains in agriculture and primary manufacturing have little statistical weight in the uptrend of the GNP series; and since the uptrend in the GNP series is stronger than the uptrend in the secondary manufacturing series, most of the relative growth in Canada must have been in the "other" sectors not identified in Chart 6.1. It is notable that upsurges in the secondary manufacturing series have usually occurred during periods of increasing protection—increases in tariffs after 1928, and the protection afforded by wartime conditions during both world wars; and that these uptrends have been followed by periods of decline during which most of the preceding gain has been lost. There is no reason, either in theory or in the empirical evidence, to think that protected manufacturing serves as a leading growth sector, except during periods of *increasing* protection—and then, of course, the growth in GNP is at the expense of growth in GNP per capita.

The data of Chart 6.1 are certainly not inconsistent with the theoretical analysis of chapters 2 and 3. "Something" in

[14]Using different data, and presenting their results in three-year moving averages, the Economic Council found the income gap to have been essentially unchanged since 1900. *Second Annual Review*, p. 51.

the Canadian economy keeps the Canadian standard of living abnormally low relative to both the American standard of living and to growth in Canadian GNP. Theory shows that effective protectionism in an open economy tends to produce just such results; the data suggest that in Canada these tendencies have been net as well as gross.

STATISTICAL APPENDIX

1. GENERAL COMMENTS

The analysis in the text is based primarily on *trends* in the Canadian : American series; the absolute values of the individual percentages are therefore of little significance for present purposes. Accordingly, in scrounging for data I have used Canadian and American figures whose trends can be relied on, even if the figures themselves are based on concepts that are not fully suited to the analysis. Similarly, the concept embodied in the figure that forms the Canadian numerator of each percentage is seldom identical with that embodied in the American denominator. For these reasons the absolute values of the percentages that are shown on the charts are not conceptually accurate measures of relative productivity, output, or earnings; they must be considered as indicating only a rough order of magnitude.

The notes that follow are intended to explain the source and character of the figures I have used in sufficient detail to allow a reader to reproduce the figures in Tables A.1 and A.2. As will be seen a large amount of arithmetic and some considerable amount of estimation lies behind the figures in these tables. From the figures given in the tables all the percentages used in the text and charts in chapters 5 and 6 may easily be calculated.

The figures in Tables A.1 and A.2 and Chart 6.1 are not adjusted for changes in the exchange rate. (It may be mentioned that I. Brecher and S. S. Reisman, in a similar comparison of Canadian and American statistics [*Canada-United States Economic Relations* (Ottawa, 1957), Appendices E and F] also make no adjustment for the exchange rate.) Changes in the exchange rate probably affect commodity-producing sectors unevenly and with a significant time lag, and a 10 per cent change in the exchange rate will, even after several years, probably change sectoral figures by considerably less than 10 per cent. In so far as exchange rate changes are reflected in domestic price changes their effects are presumably allowed for in the price deflators used to derive "volume" figures. (See footnote 3 in chapter 5.) The Hood–Scott figures used extensively in the present analysis represent constant 1949 dollars; in 1949 the Canadian dollar was at par with the American until September 19; it was then set at 90 cents American until October, 1950, when a floating rate was introduced. Our figure

131

for 1870 is probably low because the Canadian dollar was at a premium of about 12 per cent at that date, and had been at a premium for several years as a result of the Civil War inflation in the United States; the United States returned to the gold standard in 1879. The Canadian dollar was pegged at 90 cents American from September, 1939, to July, 1946. Other changes in the exchange rate, either minor or of short duration, are conveniently summarized in the *Canada Year Book 1960*, pp. 1145–7.

In charts 5.1 and 5.2 the relative earnings $(W)$ curves are adjusted by the following exchange rates, quoted in cents per U.S. dollar.

| | | |
|---|---|---|
| 1926—1.00 | 1934— .990 | 1948—1.00 |
| 1927—1.00 | 1935—1.005 | 1949—1.025* |
| 1928—1.00 | 1936—1.00 | 1950—1.089 |
| 1929—1.007 | 1937—1.00 | 1951—1.053 |
| 1930—1.002 | 1938—1.006 | 1952— .979 |
| 1931—1.038 | 1939—1.041 | 1953— .983 |
| 1932—1.135 | 1946—1.05* | 1954— .973 |
| 1933—1.087 | 1947—1.00 | 1955— .986 |

*Simple averages of monthly pegged rates and market rates.

SOURCES. 1926–39: Board of Governors of the Federal Reserve System, *Banking and Monetary Statistics* (Washington, 1943), p. 664.

1946–55: *Bank of Canada Statistical Summary Supplement 1961*, p. 143.

2. CHART 6.1

(a) *Population*

(i) Canada: official estimates, *Canada Year Book (CYB)*, various years.

(ii) United States: *Historical Statistics of the United States, Colonial Times to 1957 (Hist. Stat.)*, series A2, "Total population residing in the United States"; from 1949 on the figures used are the revised estimates for this series appearing in the *Statistical Abstract of the United States 1961*, p. 5.

(b) *Gross National Product*

(i) Canada: since 1926 official National Accounts figures for "Gross national expenditure in constant (1949) dollars" (see Dominion Bureau of Statistics, *National Accounts, Income and Expenditure, 1926–1956*, Table 5), expressed in terms of 1929 dollars; figures before 1926 are from O. J. Firestone, *Canada's Economic Development, 1867–1953* (London, 1958), p. 65, expressed in 1929 dollars by using his implicit deflator for GNP, p. 178. The Hartland estimates are from the Firestone volume, table following p. 336, and are translated into 1929 dollars by Firestone's deflator series.

(ii) United States: John W. Kendrick, *Productivity Trends in the United States* (Princeton, 1961), Table A-III, pp. 298–301, "Gross national product, commerce concept," multiplied by the 1929 GNP (p. 294). Estimates of United States GNP for 1870 and 1880 were made by adjusting Kendrick's index of "Real gross product, private

132

domestic economy" (Table A-IV, p. 303) to the GNP concept by ratios derived from Table A-III and by interpolating 1870 between the 1869 and 1879 figures and 1880 between the 1879 and 1889 figures.

(c) *Manufacturing*

(i) Canada: current dollar figures for primary and secondary manufacturing from 1870 to 1915, and 1919, from Gordon W. Bertram, "Historical Statistics on Growth and Structure of Manufacturing in Canada, 1870–1957" in J. Henripin and A. Asimakopulos, eds., *Canadian Political Science Association Conferences on Statistics 1962 and 1963* (Toronto, 1964), pp. 93–151; current dollar figures for 1917, 1918, and 1920 to 1928 are my own rough estimates, made by dividing official figures into the primary and secondary groupings. (Throughout the present work I have used Bertram's concept of primary manufacturing, which is essentially the same as that used by the *Royal Commission on Canada's Economic Prospects*; see Bertram, "Historical Statistics . . . ," p. 94. In my "Estimates of Canadian Manufacturing Output by Markets, 1870–1915" published in the Henripin and Asimakopulos volume, pp. 61–91, I have recommended a different concept of primary manufacturing which I think is preferable on theoretical grounds; see especially pp. 77–9.) No figures are shown for primary manufacturing from 1920 to 1924, because non-ferrous smelting and refining was not counted as a manufacturing industry during those years.

The current value figures are deflated by the general wholesale price index from 1870 to 1910 and by the index for fully and chiefly manufactured goods from 1915 to 1925; the indexes, on a 1926 base, are in D.B.S., *Prices and Price Indexes 1948*, Tables 1 and 4. From 1926 on, the figures are constructed by using the output indexes implicit in the figures for "Gross Domestic Product in 1949 dollars" in Wm. C. Hood and Anthony Scott, *Output, Labour and Capital in the Canadian Economy* (Ottawa, 1958), pp. 397 ff; these indexes are applied to the 1929 net value added figures for primary and secondary manufacturing as given by Bertram. (The Hood and Scott figures are based primarily on production indexes; see the discussion of the series by the authors at pp. 207–10 and 381–8.)

(ii) United States: Kendrick, *Productivity Trends . . .* , Table D-II, pp. 465–6 for output index, and p. 415 for 1929 figure.

(d) *Agriculture*

The agricultural output figures represent a "value added" or "net output" concept. They are derived from the same sources and by the same methods as were used for manufacturing. See Firestone, *Canada's Economic Development*, p. 199, for the Canadian current dollar figures 1870 to 1920; Dominion Bureau of Statistics, *Survey of Production 1926–1956*, vol. 36 (May, 1959), p. 16 (I have used the figure of .733 billion for 1929 given in this publication; later years of the publication give a revised figure of .755 billion); Hood and Scott, *Output, Labour and Capital . . .* , for the constant-dollar figures after 1926; Kendrick, *Productivity Trends . . .* , Table B-I, pp. 361–4, and p. 347 for the United States.

(e) *Rest of the Economy.* These figures are simply GNP less manufacturing output and agricultural output, as calculated above, all in 1929 dollars.

3. CHARTS 5.1 AND 5.2

The output series are from Chart 6.1.

The "productivity" series represent, in the main, output per member of the employed labour force; the divisors include proprietors, self-employed persons, etc. The Canadian figures are from Hood and Scott, *Output, Labour and Capital* . . . . The employed labour force for the residual series is the "total civilian persons with jobs" less the employed labour force in agriculture and secondary manufacturing. The United States figures for manufacturing are derived from Kendrick, *Productivity Trends* . . . , Tables DII and A-VII (p. 308); for the residual series the figures are the "Employed civilian labour force" (*Hist. Stat.*, series D5) less the sum of the agricultural labour force (series D6) less Kendrick's employment figures for manufacturing.

The "earnings" series for manufacturing is derived by dividing current dollar "wages and salaries" figures by "employees" rather than by "labour force" figures.

(i) Canada: The manufacturing series is based on the figures given in *Canada Year Book 1961*, p. 632. In order to get an estimate for secondary manufacturing we subtract from both the "employees" and "wages and salaries" figures the sum of these magnitudes for the following industries: non-ferrous metal smelting and refining; pulp and paper; slaughtering and meat packing; butter and cheese; flour and feed; sawmills; fruit and vegetable canning; and fish canning. These are the major primary manufacturing industries, though not all of them; the result of the adjustment is therefore to define a secondary manufacturing concept for the earning series that is slightly larger than the secondary manufacturing concept used in the other series. For the residual series, the numerators are the "wages, salaries and supplementary labour income" figures for the total economy less the figures for agriculture and manufacturing, as given in *National Accounts . . . 1926–1956*, Table 22, plus the wages and salaries in primary manufacturing as calculated above. The denominators for the years 1946–55 are the figures for "non-agricultural paid workers," *Canada Year Book 1961*, p. 759, less employees in manufacturing, plus employees in primary manufacturing as calculated above. The figures for employees net of primary manufacturing for 1929 to 1939 are my estimates; they were derived by comparing the labour force series for non-agricultural persons with jobs (*National Accounts . . . 1926–1956*, p. 100) less employees in all manufacturing—which should give a figure for the rest of the economy that *includes* proprietors and others—with the "non-agricultural paid workers" series less manufacturing employment—which gives the required figure for employees in the rest of the economy. The latter figure was about 76.7 per cent of the former in 1941 and 1942. On the grounds that the ratio of proprietors to employees was probably higher during the

134

thirties than in 1941, we arbitrarily take the "employees" in the rest of the economy (excluding primary manufacturing) to be 75 per cent of the figure that *includes* proprietors, self-employed persons, etc.

(ii) United States: A "wages and salaries" figure for manufacturing was estimated as follows. The "Average annual earnings per full-time employee in manufacturing" (*Hist. Stat.*, series D688 and 701) was multiplied by the figure for "Employment, full and part time" (*ibid.*, series D51); the results were compared with the wages and salaries figures from the census of manufacturing (*ibid.*, series P5) for the years for which they are available. The "gross" series was then reduced to correspond with the latter figures, and similar reduction ratios were used for the years with no census figures. The result is a crude annual series for wages and salaries; it is then divided by the "full and part time" employees series to give a series for "earnings." The numerators for the residual series are the figures for compensation of employees (*Hist. Stat.*, series F50) less our estimate for manufacturing, less wages and salaries in agriculture (*ibid.*, series K81); the denominators are the figures for civilian employees excluding farm workers (*ibid.*, series D48) less employees in manufacturing (*ibid.*, series D51).

4. ADDENDUM

The statistical work for this paper was completed before the publication by the Dominion Bureau of Statistics of the *Annual Supplement to the Monthly Index of Industrial Production* (Ottawa, May, 1963). This publication, appended to the March, 1963, issue of the *Index of Industrial Production*, provides a "Monthly quantity index of manufacturing production," in both seasonally adjusted and unadjusted forms, from 1919 to 1962 (Table 6, pp. 26–7). I have checked the annual form (unadjusted) of this index *for all manufacturing*, against the trends in my constant dollar output figures for *secondary manufacturing*. The trends in the two indexes are quite close except for the following: (*a*) our figures are considerably higher than the official figures from 1941 to 1945 inclusive (but our index for primary manufacturing output is much lower than the official index for all manufacturing from 1942 to 1945); (*b*) our figures for 1954 and 1955 are much below the official figures; the downtrend in the secondary manufacturing series in charts 5.1 and 5.2 for the years 1954 and 1955 is probably exaggerated; (*c*) the trends in the two indexes for the decade 1919 to 1929 are different, especially for the years 1924 to 1926. The slump in our Canadian output series in 1924 does not exist in the official series, which is the same in 1924 as it was in 1923; our series shows much sharper increases in 1927 and 1929 than the official series shows. Thus it is probable that the Canadian : American output series for secondary manufacturing in Chart 6.1 shows too sharp a slump from 1923 to 1926, and too sharp a rise from 1926 to 1929. Between the two years 1919 and 1928 our figures show a 60 per cent increase in output and the official figures a 55 per cent increase. It should be noted that the D.B.S. discourages use of these data "in an annual context" for the period 1919 to 1934; the reason is that "the annual levels in this period are open to question" even though the month-to-month movements are considered reliable.

TABLE A. 1
Various Series, 1870–1925

| | Population in millions | | Gross national product in billions of 1929 dollars | | Value added in manufacturing in billions of 1929 dollars | | | Value added in agriculture in billions of 1929 dollars | |
|---|---|---|---|---|---|---|---|---|---|
| | | | | | Pri-mary | Secon-dary | All | | |
| | Can. | U.S. | Can. | U.S. | Can. | Can. | U.S. | Can. | U.S. |
| 1870 | 3.63 | 39.91 | .88* | 9.40 | .036 | .105 | 2.22 | .239 | 3.70 |
| 1880 | 4.26 | 50.26 | 1.13* | 17.45 | .056 | .157 | 3.30 | .340 | 5.59 |
| 1890 | 4.78 | 63.06 | 1.57* | 26.20 | .103 | .273 | 5.92 | .425 | 6.72 |
| 1900 | 5.30 | 76.09 | 2.16* | 38.20 | .130 | .346 | 8.33 | .594 | 8.64 |
| 1910 | 6.99 | 92.41 | 3.55 | 56.50 | .243 | .603 | 13.56 | .853 | 9.42 |
| 1915 | 7.98 | 100.55 | 4.15 | 60.42 | .203 | .525 | 18.01 | | |
| 6 | 8.00 | 101.97 | 4.32 | 68.87 | | | | | |
| 7 | 8.06 | 103.27 | 4.40 | 67.26 | .254 | .796 | 21.22 | | |
| 8 | 8.15 | 103.20 | 4.45 | 73.36 | .260 | .760 | 20.98 | | |
| 9 | 8.31 | 104.51 | 4.55 | 74.16 | .311 | .705 | 18.34 | | |
| 1920 | 8.56 | 106.47 | 4.42 | 73.31 | | .704 | 19.84 | .672 | 9.55 |
| 1 | 8.79 | 108.54 | 4.03 | 71.58 | | .685 | 16.08 | | |
| 2 | 8.92 | 110.06 | 4.35 | 75.79 | | .769 | 20.47 | | |
| 3 | 9.01 | 111.95 | 4.51 | 85.82 | | .805 | 23.12 | | |
| 4 | 9.14 | 114.11 | 4.51 | 88.36 | | .721 | 22.07 | | |
| 1925 | 9.29 | 115.83 | 4.82 | 90.53 | .294 | .753 | 24.62 | | |

*The Hartland figures for these years are: .71, 1.00, 1.40 and 2.03.

5. EXAMPLE RE TABLE A.2: HOW TO FIND THE PERCENTAGES GIVEN FOR 1935 IN CHART 5.2
Residual output for Canada is GNP minus Value added in Agriculture and Secondary manufacturing, i.e., 5.20 — .76 — 1.09 = 3.35 billions. Dividing this figure by the Residual labour force, 1.98 millions, gives us the Canadian productivity figure of approximately $1692. The Canadian Earnings figure is the wages and salaries figure, $1.55 billions divided by the Employees figure of 1.55 millions, or $1000. The $W/M$ figure for Canada is accordingly .59.

For the United States, Residual output is 91.4 — 24.9 — 10.4 = 56.1 billions, and Productivity 56.1 ÷ 23.2 = $2418 approximately. The Earnings figure is 26.9 billion ÷ 17.9 million, or $1503 approximately. The $W/M$ figure is therefore approximately .62.

The percentage that the Canadian $W/M$ figure bears to the American $W/M$ figure is therefore (.59/.62) × 100 or about 95.1. This is

136

Various Series, 1926–1955

| | Population in millions | | Gross national product in billions of 1929 dollars | | Value added in manufacturing in billions of 1929 dollars | | |
|---|---|---|---|---|---|---|---|
| | | | | | Primary | Secondary | All |
| | Can. | U.S. | Can. | U.S. | Can. | Can. | U.S. |
| 1926 | 9.45 | 117.4 | 5.13 | 96.4 | .380 | 1.04 | 25.9 |
| 7 | 9.64 | 119.0 | 5.60 | 97.3 | .393 | 1.13 | 26.2 |
| 8 | 9.84 | 120.5 | 6.12 | 98.5 | .424 | 1.23 | 27.1 |
| 9 | 10.03 | 121.8 | 6.13 | 104.4 | .438 | 1.32 | 30.1 |
| 30 | 10.21 | 123.1 | 5.88 | 95.1 | .417 | 1.17 | 25.6 |
| 1931 | 10.38 | 124.0 | 5.12 | 89.5 | .345 | 1.03 | 21.6 |
| 2 | 10.51 | 124.8 | 4.60 | 76.4 | .301 | .86 | 16.2 |
| 3 | 10.63 | 125.6 | 4.31 | 74.2 | .323 | .84 | 18.9 |
| 4 | 10.74 | 126.4 | 4.83 | 80.8 | .382 | .99 | 20.8 |
| 5 | 10.85 | 127.3 | 5.20 | 91.4 | .417 | 1.09 | 24.9 |
| 1936 | 10.95 | 128.1 | 5.43 | 100.9 | .470 | 1.21 | 29.1 |
| 7 | 11.05 | 128.8 | 5.97 | 109.1 | .525 | 1.39 | 31.1 |
| 8 | 11.15 | 129.8 | 6.01 | 103.2 | .482 | 1.26 | 24.3 |
| 9 | 11.27 | 130.9 | 6.46 | 111.0 | .525 | 1.34 | 30.8 |
| 40 | 11.38 | 132.0 | 7.39 | 121.0 | .621 | 1.73 | 35.7 |
| 1941 | 11.51 | 133.1 | 8.45 | 138.7 | .731 | 2.35 | 47.5 |
| 2 | 11.65 | 133.9 | 10.36 | 154.7 | .785 | 3.00 | 59.3 |
| 3 | 11.80 | 134.2 | 10.44 | 170.2 | .810 | 3.33 | 71.6 |
| 4 | 11.95 | 132.9 | 10.8 | 183.6 | .828 | 3.48 | 69.9 |
| 5 | 12.07 | 132.5 | 10.5 | 180.9 | .793 | 2.90 | 59.1 |
| 1946 | 12.29 | 140.1 | 10.3 | 165.6 | .831 | 2.43 | 48.3 |
| 7 | 12.55 | 143.4 | 10.5 | 164.1 | .908 | 2.62 | 53.6 |
| 8 | 12.82 | 146.1 | 10.7 | 173.0 | .935 | 2.71 | 55.4 |
| 9 | 13.45 | 148.7 | 11.1 | 170.6 | .941 | 2.75 | 52.2 |
| 50 | 13.71 | 151.2 | 11.8 | 187.4 | .996 | 2.89 | 60.5 |
| 1951 | 14.01 | 153.4 | 12.6 | 199.4 | 1.07 | 3.10 | 64.4 |
| 2 | 14.46 | 155.8 | 13.6 | 205.8 | 1.07 | 3.18 | 67.2 |
| 3 | 14.85 | 158.3 | 14.1 | 214.0 | 1.11 | 3.47 | 73.2 |
| 4 | 15.29 | 161.2 | 13.7 | 208.6 | 1.15 | 3.18 | 68.6 |
| 5 | 15.70 | 164.3 | 14.8 | 225.6 | 1.23 | 3.41 | 76.9 |

the figure that appears on Chart 5.2. The relative Output figure is
(3.35/56.1) $\times$ 100, or 5.97 per cent; the relative Productivity figure
(1692/2418) $\times$ 100, or 70 per cent; and the relative Earnings figure
(1000/1503) $\times$ 100, or 66.5 per cent. (I have used more decimal
places in the actual calculations, and the percentages charted for 1935
are actually: $WM/M$, 95.5 unadjusted for the exchange rate and 95.1
adjusted; $O$, 5.96; $M$, 69.6; and $W$, 66.5 unadjusted and 66.2
adjusted.)

137

| | Value added in agriculture in billions of 1929 dollars | | Employed labour force in millions | | | |
|---|---|---|---|---|---|---|
| | | | Manufacturing | | Residual sector* | |
| | Can. | U.S. | Secondary Can. | All U.S. | Can. | U.S. |
| 1926 | .92 | 10.3 | .50 | 10.0 | | |
| 7 | .98 | 10.6 | .51 | 9.9 | | |
| 8 | 1.03 | 10.4 | .55 | 9.9 | | |
| 9 | .73 | 10.7 | .59 | 10.6 | 2.01 | 26.6 |
| 30 | .89 | 10.0 | .56 | 9.4 | 1.99 | 25.7 |
| 1931 | .74 | 11.2 | .51 | 8.0 | 1.91 | 24.1 |
| 2 | .89 | 10.7 | .45 | 6.8 | 1.74 | 22.0 |
| 3 | .64 | 11.0 | .44 | 7.3 | 1.77 | 21.4 |
| 4 | .70 | 9.5 | .48 | 8.5 | 1.90 | 22.5 |
| 5 | .76 | 10.4 | .52 | 9.0 | 1.98 | 23.2 |
| 1936 | .70 | 9.8 | .53 | 9.8 | 2.06 | 24.7 |
| 7 | .68 | 10.9 | .57 | 10.7 | 2.18 | 25.8 |
| 8 | .86 | 11.4 | .56 | 9.2 | 2.08 | 25.3 |
| 9 | .99 | 11.5 | .57 | 10.1 | 2.12 | 26.1 |
| 40 | 1.02 | 11.4 | | | | |
| 1941 | .87 | 12.3 | | | | |
| 2 | 1.29 | 13.2 | | | | |
| 3 | .87 | 12.6 | | | | |
| 4 | 1.07 | 12.7 | | | | |
| 5 | .81 | 12.2 | | | | |
| 1946 | .90 | 12.4 | .96 | 14.7 | 2.55 | 32.2 |
| 7 | .83 | 11.9 | .99 | 15.4 | 2.73 | 34.3 |
| 8 | .89 | 12.8 | .99 | 15.5 | 2.80 | 35.9 |
| 9 | .86 | 12.7 | 1.03 | 14.4 | 2.84 | 36.3 |
| 50 | .95 | 12.9 | 1.04 | 15.2 | 2.94 | 37.3 |
| 1951 | 1.06 | 12.2 | 1.05 | 16.3 | 3.12 | 37.6 |
| 2 | 1.16 | 12.2 | 1.05 | 16.6 | 3.24 | 37.9 |
| 3 | 1.09 | 13.1 | 1.09 | 17.4 | 3.30 | 38.2 |
| 4 | .87 | 13.6 | 1.01 | 16.2 | 3.31 | 38.5 |
| 5 | 1.06 | 14.3 | 1.05 | 16.8 | 3.46 | 39.7 |

| | Employees in millions | | | | Wages and salaries in billions of current dollars | | | |
|---|---|---|---|---|---|---|---|---|
| | Manufacturing | | Residual Sector* | | Manufacturing | | Residual sector* | |
| | Secondary Can. | All U.S. | Can. | U.S. | Secondary Can. | All U.S. | Can. | U.S. |
| 1926 | .43 | 10.0 | | | .496 | 13.4 | | |
| 7 | .46 | 9.8 | | | .529 | 13.3 | | |
| 8 | .49 | 9.8 | | | .584 | 13.2 | | |
| 9 | .52 | 10.5 | 1.54 | 20.5 | .633 | 14.3 | 2.18 | 35.5 |
| 30 | .48 | 9.4 | 1.51 | 19.7 | .570 | 12.3 | 2.10 | 33.3 |
| 1931 | .44 | 8.0 | 1.54 | 18.4 | .486 | 9.7 | 1.83 | 29.1 |
| 2 | .38 | 6.8 | 1.41 | 16.6 | .393 | 6.9 | 1.51 | 23.5 |
| 3 | .38 | 7.3 | 1.38 | 16.2 | .357 | 6.9 | 1.37 | 22.0 |
| 4 | .42 | 8.3 | 1.53 | 17.4 | .408 | 8.5 | 1.46 | 25.1 |
| 5 | .45 | 8.9 | 1.55 | 17.9 | .453 | 9.6 | 1.55 | 26.9 |
| 1936 | .48 | 9.7 | 1.60 | 19.1 | .493 | 10.9 | 1.66 | 31.1 |
| 7 | .53 | 10.6 | 1.72 | 20.1 | .579 | 12.8 | 1.87 | 34.1 |
| 8 | .52 | 9.3 | 1.67 | 19.6 | .569 | 10.8 | 1.85 | 33.2 |
| 9 | .53 | 10.1 | 1.69 | 20.2 | .596 | 12.6 | 1.93 | 34.5 |
| 40 | | | | | | | | |
| 1941 | | | | | | | | |
| 2 | | | | | | | | |
| 3 | | | | | | | | |
| 4 | | | | | | | | |
| 5 | | | | | | | | |
| 1946 | .87 | 14.5 | 2.12 | 26.8 | 1.430 | 33.9 | 4.18 | 81.3 |
| 7 | .94 | 15.3 | 2.20 | 28.2 | 1.702 | 39.7 | 4.53 | 86.3 |
| 8 | .95 | 15.3 | 2.28 | 29.1 | 1.964 | 43.3 | 5.26 | 94.7 |
| 9 | .96 | 14.2 | 2.36 | 29.1 | 2.124 | 40.8 | 5.76 | 97.1 |
| 50 | .97 | 15.0 | 2.46 | 29.7 | 2.269 | 46.4 | 6.24 | 105.0 |
| 1951 | 1.03 | 16.1 | 2.59 | 31.2 | 2.666 | 54.6 | 7.36 | 122.8 |
| 2 | 1.06 | 16.3 | 2.74 | 32.0 | 2.984 | 59.4 | 8.20 | 132.8 |
| 3 | 1.10 | 17.2 | 2.74 | 32.5 | 3.273 | 66.7 | 8.85 | 139.3 |
| 4 | 1.04 | 16.0 | 2.79 | 32.4 | 3.177 | 62.9 | 9.33 | 142.0 |
| 5 | 1.06 | 16.6 | 2.92 | 33.5 | 3.369 | 68.8 | 9.93 | 152.4 |

*The Residual Sector is the non-agricultural, non-manufacturing sector in the United States; in Canada it is the non-agricultural, non-secondary manufacturing sector.

# III

# 7

## Canada's National Policies

To the infant industry argument for protectionism Canadians have added an infant nation argument. Among Canadian academic historians, journalists, and citizens at large there seems to be a dangerous unanimity of opinion that Canada is a transparently artificial entity whose very existence has always depended on something called a national policy. Canada, in this view, is a denial of geography and a travesty of economics that stands as living proof of the primacy of politics in the affairs of men. Critical comment to the effect that most Canadian manufacturers still depend on protective tariffs is very apt to be greeted first by astonishment that anyone would think the comment worth making, and then by patient explanation that of course many parts of the Canadian economy—not only manufacturing—have *always* depended on government bounty in one form or another, and that Canada simply would not exist as a nation if public support were not continuously made available to key sectors of the economy. Such a policy is necessary, the explanation continues, both in order to overcome the outrageous geography of the country and in order to defend the nation's economy against the formidable efficiency, and thus the natural expansionism, of the American economy. In Canada infant industries are not *expected* to grow up.

I reject this view of Canada. It seems to me to be subversive not only of the nation's wealth but also of the nation's pride. National pride and economic performance I believe to be positively, not negatively, correlated; both efficiency and honour, as the parable of the talents teaches, come from making the most of what one has, not from having the most. And yet Canadian economic policy—and, what is more important, the economic policy of so many developing nations today—aims consistently at maximizing the purse, gross national product, rather than the performance, gross national product per citizen.

Sir John A. Macdonald gave us our first national policy, and our first lessons in the irrelevance of economics. Western lands, he argued, must be controlled by the Dominion because provincial land policies "might be obstructive to immigration," i.e., provinces might actually try to sell land rather than give it away. Canadian railways, in Macdonald's view, were not to be thought of primarily as business enterprises; they were instruments of national development and served this end by providing both attractive objects of government expenditure and reliable sources of party support. As for the tariff, Macdonald rang all the changes on the protectionist fallacies and promised that *his* tariff would benefit everyone, the teachings of the dismal science notwithstanding. Macdonald was the first great Canadian non-economist.

It is hard to believe, though, that Macdonald deserves the whole credit for the low esteem in which economics and economists are held in Canada today. Macdonald has in any event had powerful support from Canadian historians, of both the political and economic persuasions, who have rationalized his national policy and have encouraged Canadians to believe that by disregarding economics they could build a nation that would represent a victory over mere materialism. The national policy originally consisted of government support for three main ventures: railway building, Western settlement, and manufacturing development. (We adopt the original convention of using "national policy" for the famous trinity of Canadian nation-building policies, and of reserving "National Policy" for the protective tariff policy.) The mutual consistency of Western settlement and railway building was perhaps fairly obvious; land grants helped to finance railways, and railway companies encouraged settlement. From an economist's point of view, however, the rationalization has been

144

carried a little far. The government has been praised for using valuable lands as a loss-leader, while the C.P.R. has been praised for selling land to immigrants at prices considerably below those charged by other land owners, and for showing great initiative in developing uneconomic irrigation projects.

What was at first difficult for historians to discover was the consistency between Macdonald's tariff policy and the other two prongs of his national policy. The late Professor H. A. Innis seems to have provided the connecting argument. The role of the tariff in the Canadian economy, he taught, was to inhibit Canadian-American trade, to promote east-west trade in Canada, and in this way to provide revenue for Canadian transcontinental railways. Though I cannot resist a long footnote on the subject, I do not want to make a full textual analysis of Innis' writings in order to try to find out whether he believed that his tariff-railway link was (*a*) the *ex post* result of the two policies—the way things worked out—or (*b*) the *ex-ante* design—the way things were intended to work out—or (*c*) either or both of these combined with the opinion that the link was felicitous.[1] I wish only to suggest that once the Innis link was forged the way was wide open for a

[1]The Innis link was derived from Galt's argument, made in reply to protests from British manufacturers against his raising of the Canadian tariff in the late 1850s, that increased tariff revenue was necessary to help pay for Canadian canals and railways that could not be profitably built by private concerns, and that British manufacturers ought to be pleased with the arrangement because the cheaper cost of transportation would lower the price of British manufactured goods in Canada and thus increase the market for them. Innis accepted as profound this economic doubletalk of a suave politician, though with a certain amount of incredulity about its source: ". . . whether or not [Galt's] explanation was one of rationalization after the fact, or of original theoretical analysis, reliance on the customs was undoubtedly the only solution." Surely it was not the only solution; if the canals had been paid for by domestic taxation, or by import duties that were no heavier than domestic excise duties, the British manufacturers would have been at least as well off, and Canadians would have been better off. A subsidy is always to be preferred to a tariff on both economic grounds and political grounds; on economic grounds because direct payments distort resource allocation less than indirect payments, and on political grounds because direct payments involve less deception than indirect payments.

Galt was talking *mainly* of revenue tariffs. Innis extended the Galt argument to tariffs that were mainly protective, and thereby compounded Galt's error. "The National Policy was designed not only to increase revenue from customs [as in Galt's argument] but also to increase revenue from traffic from the standpoint of the railways. The increasing importance

145

full-scale rationalization of the national policy. Thus D. G. Creighton:

[The tariff] was intimately and vitally related to the other national policies. By means of the tariff, the settlement of the west would provide a national market; and this national market would supply east-west traffic for Canadian transcontinental railways and areas of exploitation for eastern Canadian industry.[2]

And J. B. Brebner:

Looking backward from the present, it is easy to see that the very existence of both the Province and the later Dominion of Canada as entities separate from the United States has depended on such expensive transportation services that a large proportion of their cost has had to be met from the public purse. . . . it was [in the exuberant 1850s] that Canadians . . . began systematically to adopt the *only* procedure by which they could surmount this handicap, that is, the imposition of quite high tariffs on manufactured goods.[3]

---

of railways has tended to emphasize the position of protection rather than revenue." As economic theory this is absurd, not only because the railways, like the canals, could have been financed more efficiently by subsidy than by tariff, but also because a tariff cannot at the same time maximize both protection and revenue; the greater the protective effect of a tariff the less the revenue will provide. The charitable interpretation of this passage is that Innis was indulging in "rationalization after the fact." In the article in which these passages occurred, Innis at any rate doubted the *future* application of his argument: "Dependence on the application of mature technique, especially in transport, to virgin natural resources must steadily recede in importance as a basis for the tariff. It will become increasingly difficult to wield the tariff as the crude but effective weapon by which we have been able to obtain a share of our natural resources."

All of the above quotations are taken from an article by Innis published in 1931, and reprinted in H. A. Innis, *Essays in Canadian Economic History* (Toronto, 1956), pp. 76–7. Two years later Innis was in a deep quandary about the effect of the Canadian tariff. "Inflexibility of the tariff downward contributed to the difficulties during the period of prosperity which began . . . in 1896 . . ." (*ibid.*, p. 91). On the following page he wrote that "During a period of prosperity the tariff should be raised to act as a brake. . . . If railroad rates are lowered at the beginning of a period of prosperity tariff rates should be raised accordingly. . . . Lowering the tariff during the period of a depression and raising the tariff during a period of prosperity might do much to alleviate the problem of a staple-producing area" (p. 92–3). The only way I can see of resolving the contradiction between these two quotations is to suppose that in the first Innis was thinking of the combined effect on C.P.R. revenues of the wheat boom and the continued support of the tariff, and the consequent effect of swollen railway revenues in promoting a new, and uneconomically large, railway building program in Canada: had the tariff been lowered, and the C.P.R.'s profits thereby dampened, the incentive to build *two* new transcontinental railways in Canada would have been reduced; and that in the

## W. T. Easterbrook and H. G. Aitken:

[The detailed program of Canadian nation building] appeared slowly and in piecemeal fashion but by 1879 . . . the parts of the comprehensive and more or less complete pattern had fallen into place: a transcontinental railway, protective tariffs, land settlement policy, the promotion of immigration.[4]

And the present author, who providentially has written very little on the subject:

The Dominion immediately proceeded to fulfil its purposes. A transcontinental railway system was constructed, an energetic settlement policy was adapted to the needs of the West, and the tariff was designed to develop Canadian industry and stimulate Canadian trade. These policies proved effective in the period of prosperity which began towards the end of the nineteenth century.[5]

Two features of the historians' stereotype of the national policy should be noted. First, much emphasis is placed on the consistency of the three pillars of the program, while inconsistencies are either ignored or glossed over. Among the

---

second he was thinking of the Western farmer: the wheat boom might have been dampened by raising farm cost by means of *increased* tariff rates in order to offset the advantages that farmers gained by lowered railway rates. Since the final part of the second quotation recommends a counter-cyclical tariff policy (Innis must have known how politically impracticable *this* was!), with no qualification about how railway rates should be changed, one can only make sense out of this passage by supposing that by 1933 Innis was willing to sacrifice the railways to the farmers during depression and the farmers to the railways during prosperity; his recommended policy would be counter-cyclical for farmers and pro-cyclical for railways! Perhaps the subtlety, or the confusion, was covering a retreat. Realizing that a high tariff may "become inadequate" during depressions (p. 91), and suggesting that the period of resource expansion in Canada had ended, Innis in fact repudiated his linking of the National Policy and railways by reverting to the lesser economic confusions of Galt's position: "Assuming relative stability in the production of raw materials as a result of exhaustion of natural resources the tariff must assume to an increasing extent the position of a toll, as Galt originally planned, and should approximate the deficit on transportation finance" (p. 93). Unfortunately the damage had been done, for textbook writers cannot spare the time to assess qualifications to, or second thoughts on, powerful generalizations.
[2]*Dominion of the North* (Toronto, 1944), p. 346.
[3]*North Atlantic Triangle* (New Haven and Toronto, 1945), p. 158. My italics.
[4]*Canadian Economic History* (Toronto, 1956), p. 383.
[5]*Engineering and Society*, Part II (Toronto, 1946), p. 246.

147

authors I have consulted, several mention the regional inconsistency inherent in the policy. V. C. Fowke, in particular, interpreted the national policy as a program designed by and for central Canadians. The national policy is therefore seen not as national at all but rather as a policy of central Canadian imperialism. Fowke comes dangerously close to shattering the whole myth of the national policy, yet in the end he refuses to be an iconoclast. Thus his glosses that the national policy was "prerequisite to western development" and that "the groundwork [for western development] . . . was laid . . . by the institution of the 'National Policy' of tariff protection . . ."[6] seem wildly inconsistent with his main position, particularly in view of his insistence that Macdonald's railway policy was *not* prerequisite to western development: "As far as the western provinces are concerned . . . Canadian railways are expensive alternatives to American railways rather than to no railways at all."[7] Brebner and Careless both hint at the logical inconsistency inherent in protectionism, namely, the attempt to build a wealthy nation by lowering the standard of living of its population. Thus Careless notes that "A protective tariff plainly meant that goods would cost more to buy in Canada," yet after a token flirtation with this line of reasoning he surrenders to the stereotype on the following page and concludes that "as far as Canada is concerned the protective tariff system that was adopted under Macdonald . . . did much in the long run to develop the wealth and encourage the industry of the Dominion."[8] He then goes on to paint the usual picture of the wonderful consistency among Canada's railway, settlement, and tariff policies.

None of the authors I have examined has flatly challenged the national stereotype of the beneficence of the national policy. W. A. Mackintosh, however, writes very cautiously

[6]*Canadian Agricultural Policy* (Toronto, 1946), p. 8. Fowke may mean that the national policy was a prerequisite from central Canadians' point of view, i.e., that central Canada would not have "invested" in the West without it. At the same time he would not argue that eastern investment was a *sine qua non* of western development; see note 7.
[7]V. C. Fowke, *The National Policy and the Wheat Economy* (Toronto, 1957), p. 69.
[8]J. M. S. Careless, *Canada* (Toronto, 1953), pp. 277–8.

about this subject. He outlines the "Basic National Decisions" and their interrelations in chapter II of his *The Economic Background of Dominion-Provincial Relations*,[9] but adds at the end of the chapter (p. 21): "It is not suggested that these national decisions were taken by governments, or still less by electorates, in full consciousness of their implications, nor that the inter-relations among them were fully appreciated. They were in large measure the outcome of conflicts of interest and, to some extent, of political expediency." Later (p. 37) he notes the regional conflicts occasioned by the national policies, and the tendency of these policies to rigidify the economy by creating "vested interests, regional and sectional, which would resist readjustment." Also two other authors, both political historians, have distinguished themselves by refusing to have anything to do with the standard patter. Chester Martin disdains even to mention the tariff in his *Foundations of Canadian Nationhood*[10]; A. R. M. Lower bluntly refers to the National Policy as being a "frank creation of vested manufacturing interests living on the bounty of government," and in exasperation writes that "Macdonald's way of imposing the new tariff was simple: he just invited anyone who wanted a duty to come to Ottawa and ask for it."[11]

The stereotype of the national policy is powerful enough not only to bridge logical inconsistencies but also to abridge time. To its defenders the national policy was both a well-designed and a powerful engine of nation-building. Yet it refused to function for some twenty or thirty years. Many authors simply ignore this awkward gap in timing, as I did myself in the quotation above. Others mention it and then ignore it, as for example Easterbrook and Aitken: "The three decades following Confederation . . . seemed to many a prolonged period of marking time . . . Not until the turn of the century did the program of nation-building begin to pay off . . ." (p. 381). After a long account of the Time of Troubles in both its economic and political aspects, Careless finds himself concluding that "conservative nationalism was

9Ottawa, 1939.    10Toronto, 1956.
11*Colony to Nation* (Toronto, 1946), pp. 373–4.

149

played out," and thus in imminent danger of rending the stereotype beyond repair. But he draws back at the very brink of the abyss, and proclaims in strident tones that "Macdonald nationalism had not failed. It was the age that had failed . . ." (p. 295).

Why can we not bring ourselves to say quite simply that the national policy was a dismal failure? Everyone admits, for example, that the land settlement policy was a failure before 1900. After 1900 the demand for western land was so brisk, and the C.P.R. and various land companies so zealous in attracting settlers to the region, that it is hard to believe that the homestead policy was in any sense necessary as a means of settling the West. It was, indeed, probably undesirable. After writing of the efficiency and enterprise of the private land companies, Martin notes that "The general opening of 'Dominion lands,' even- and odd-numbered sections alike, to homestead entry after 1908 brought a deluge of less selective migration to Western Canada. In vain the government had sought to reserve vast areas with marginal rainfall in 'Palliser's triangle' for grazing and other purposes. In the queues which formed up at the land offices prospective settlers, as one observer records, 'held their place in the line day and night for two or three weeks to enable them to file on certain lands,' and places in the queue were frequently bought and sold for 'substantial sums of money.' " Uneconomically low prices inevitably produce queues. No one, I suggest, really believes that without the homestead policy in particular, and the settlement policy in general, the West would not have been settled. These policies were powerless to promote settlement before 1900; after 1900 their chief effect was to promote not settlement but *rapid* settlement, and there is much evidence to suggest that the rapidity of settlement did much short-term and long-term harm in Western Canada. Martin's trenchant criticism of the homestead system certainly permits one to believe that Canada would have been better off without this member of the national policy trilogy.

As with land settlement policy so with tariff policy; the burden of the argument in previous chapters suggests that

150

we would have been much better off still if we had never tangled with the National Policy. Historically it need only be noted that manufacturing was developing in Canada well before the tariff of 1879; Mackintosh notes that the "Census of 1871 reveals that Canada had made some progress along the path of industrialization," and that "The new protectionist policy intensified, broadly speaking, industrial trends already visible."[12] Moreover, Canadian manufacturing grew less rapidly than American manufacturing both before and after the tariff and net emigration from Canada was a feature of the decades both before and after 1879. To the extent that the National Policy was intended to reverse, or even to reduce, the disparity in Canadian and American growth rates it was clearly a failure. After 1900 the Canadian economy, including Canadian manufacturing, grew more rapidly than the American economy for a dozen years, and Canadian historians have not hesitated to attribute this surge to the beneficial, if somewhat delayed, effects of the National Policy. As Careless wrote,[13] it was the "age that had failed" before 1900 and the rise of a prosperous age after 1900 that "spelt success at long last for the National Policy. . . ." In Canadian history it is heads the National Policy wins, and tails the age loses.

There remains the curious case of the C.P.R. While a Canadian transcontinental railway, as Fowke argues, was not prerequisite to western development, economists and political scientists can agree that as a matter of political economy such a railway was an essential adjunct of nationhood for the new Dominion. The railway had to be built for political reasons, whatever the subsidy involved; sensible economic policy required only that the subsidy be kept as low as possible. The C.P.R. was in fact heavily subsidized. Still, given the lacklustre performance of Canadian settlement and tariff policies before the middle 1890s one might have expected, on the basis of the national policy stereotype in general and the Innis link in particular, that the C.P.R. would have been unable

[12]*The Economic Background of Dominion-Provincial Relations*, pp. 17 and 20.
[13]*Canada*, pp. 295 and 312.

151

to survive its first bleak decade. Surely no one would wish to argue that the population of Western Canada in 1895 (perhaps a third of a million people, an increase of something over 100,000 since the completion of the C.P.R.) was able to supply either enough wheat or a large enough market for manufactured goods to make a paying proposition out of even so heavily subsidized a transcontinental railway as the C.P.R. Yet the C.P.R. was profitable from the minute it was completed and began to pay dividends on its common stock in 1889. The Wheat Boom that began in the closing years of the century was only the frosting on the cake that allowed the Company to raise dividends from 4% in 1897 to 10% in 1911, despite large decreases in railway rates around the turn of the century. The chronology of C.P.R. earnings thus raises a nagging doubt about whether the C.P.R. ever *needed* to be subsidized indirectly by the tariff as well as directly by grants of money and a kingdom in land. Professor Fogel's conclusion that the Union Pacific Railway would have been profitable *without* subsidies, despite unanimous opinion, before the fact, that it would not be,[14] suggests a need for testing the hypothesis that the C.P.R. would have been profitable with direct subsidies alone, or even, subversive thought, without *any* subsidy! Careful analysis of this matter seems to be an urgent necessity. The core of the national policy has always been the protective tariff, and although today the tariff is more and more often brazenly defended simply on the grounds that we must protect the vested interests we have built up, the argument of last resort is still that the tariff is the defender of the railways, and thus of the east-west economy. The defence retains its appeal since the railways still carry a great deal of freight, if not many passengers, and the Innis link remains persuasive. If it were possible to deny the validity of the Innis argument that without the tariff there would be no C.P.R., it would be much more difficult for present-day nationalists to argue that if there were no tariff there would be no Canada.

There are, therefore, reasonable grounds for questioning the validity of the historians' stereotype of the national policy.

[14]R. W. Fogel, *The Union Pacific Railroad* (Baltimore, 1960), *passim*.

To stress the consistency of the national policy as an inter-related whole is to ignore all too cavalierly its inconsistencies. And to write as if the wisdom and power of a nation-building program that is ineffective for two or three decades is somehow "proved" or "demonstrated" by a subsequent period of great prosperity is to mislead the public with a monstrous example of the *post hoc ergo propter hoc* fallacy. Moreover, the whole tortuous exercise is so unnecessary, for a much more reasonable, and very much simpler, explanation of the Great Canadian Boom is also standard fare in our textbooks. This explanation runs in terms of a number of world events and developments in the last decade of the nineteenth century, all of which reacted favourably on the Canadian economy—the "closing" of the American frontier, rising world prices, falling shipping rates, the development of the gradual reduction process for milling wheat, and the development of the technique of making paper from wood pulp are perhaps the principal items in the list. None of these factors owed anything to the national policy.

Why, then, do historians insist on overdetermining their explanation of the Great Boom by trying to fit a perfectly straightforward argument into the national policy stereotype, as Fowke, for example, does when he writes that "This conjuncture of world circumstances created the opportunity for Canadian expansion, but a half-century of foundation work along the lines of the national policy had prepared Canada for the opportunity."[15] Economic man does not need to be prepared by government policy before he reacts to opportunities for making profits. Is it crude hero worship, or an unconscious human predisposition to human explanations of history that leads Canadians to believe that what success they have enjoyed "must" reflect Macdonald's wise nation-building policies? Or are we all of us merely prisoners of our own history—as it has been written? It is very odd that, enjoying one of the highest standards of living in the world, Canadians in all walks of life should nevertheless believe that their economy is a frail, hothouse creation, whose very survival depends on the constant vigilance of a government gardener

[15]*The National Policy and the Wheat Economy*, p. 70.

well provided with props and plant food. Who but historians could have created this chasm between reality and belief? It is high time that someone should write the history of Canada since Confederation as a triumph of the forces of economic and political development over the national policies of Macdonald and his successors.

## II

Our national policies were laid down when Canada was young, both politically and economically. The country looked forward to a long period of what I shall call *extensive* economic growth—a combination of geographical expansion, immigration, the exploitation of new resources, railway building, and the extension of manufacturing and service industries to keep pace with the growth of the national economy. The national policies were adopted to facilitate this "natural" growth process; they were designed to increase natural resources through political expansion, human resources through immigration, social capital by railway building, and private capital by means of the tariff. This "vision" of growth was surely not unreasonable in 1870, even though, as things turned out, it failed to materialize during the next generation. In retrospect it is easy enough to see why the expectation was premature: world demand for wheat had not yet grown to the point where, even with rail transportation, wheat could be profitably exported from the Canadian prairies; technology had not yet released the wealth of the Canadian shield in terms of base metals, pulpwood, and waterpower; and the absence of cheap coal and iron ore hampered manufacturing development. It was only with the "conjuncture" around 1900 that natural economic expansion gave the national policies something to facilitate. For a generation thereafter, extensive growth was the stuff of Canadian economic development.

Extensive growth, which is essentially a process of increasing the quantity of resources, provides the sort of massive economic development that fascinates economic historians.

154

Yet from an economic point of view it is such a simple type of growth that it holds almost no interest for economic theorists, who concern themselves primarily with the efficient use of *a given quantity* of resources, and who therefore tend to think of economic progress not in terms of amassing resources but in terms of making better use of existing resources. Fortunately, however, economic historians and economic theorists *do* have a common interest in an improvement of resource *quality* as a third path to the wealth of nations. Historians have long manifested an interest in technological change, which may be considered as a means of improving the quality of capital resources, and in such things as health, diet, training, and a wide range of institutional factors that affect the quality of human resources. Only recently have economic theorists invaded in force the fields of technology, health, education, recreation, and governmental activities, but already the power of economic analysis is beginning to make itself felt in public policies relating to these matters.

Both better resource allocation and resource improvement, but especially the latter, result in what I shall call *intensive* economic growth, a type of growth that has little to do with the mere multiplying of resources that is the basic characteristic of extensive economic growth. Intensive growth, as against extensive growth, involves better job opportunities rather than more job opportunities, more highly trained people rather than more people, better use of capital and land rather than more capital and land—in brief, a better performance rather than a larger one. Extensive growth implies primary concern with the GNP growth rate; intensive growth implies primary concern with the GNP per capita growth rate. What must now be asked is whether the rough-hewn concepts of extensive and intensive growth have any operational significance, and if so whether national policies designed for extensive growth have any place in an age of intensive growth.

It is, of course, true that it would be hard to find historical examples of either pure intensive or pure extensive growth.

155

The important question is whether it is legitimate to charac-
terize certain periods as periods of *predominantly* intensive
or extensive growth. Both traditional history and Professor
Gallman's quantitative work suggest that for the United States
it is meaningful to distinguish between the extensive growth
of the last half of the nineteenth century and the intensive
growth of the first half of the twentieth. Thus Gallman found
that "the rate of increase of commodity output over the first
fifty years of the twentieth century was very far below the rate
for the last sixty years of the nineteenth," but "the average
rate of change of commodity output per capita was about the
same in the twentieth as in the nineteenth century."[16] That
twentieth-century economic growth in the United States has
been mainly of the *intensive* variety is made clear by Gallman's findings that "the twentieth century average decade
rate of increase of gainful workers in commodity production
was only . . . slightly more than one-fifth as large as that of
the nineteenth. The twentieth century increases in commodity
output were largely productivity increases. . . . Productivity
advance in commodity production was sufficiently high to
maintain a high rate of growth of commodity output per
member of the population, despite the fact that a sharply
declining share of the population was engaged in commodity
production."[17]

In Canada we have only the beginnings of a statistical
history of our economic growth before 1926 and we cannot
with confidence argue from the statistical record. Nevertheless the Canadian GNP data given in the appendix to chapter
6, based on Firestone's figures for the pre-1926 period, fail
to show any evidence of retardation in the growth of GNP
since 1900, or even since 1880, and clearly suggest some
modest acceleration of GNP growth in the period since the
Second World War. Taken at face value—and I find it hard
to believe that the general trends of the data are misleading—
the suggestion is that Canada has remained in a period of

[16] R. E. Gallman "Commodity Output, 1839–1899" in *Trends in the American Economy in the Nineteenth Century* (Princeton, 1960), pp. 18 and 20.
[17] *Ibid.*, p. 20.

extensive economic growth for the past sixty or seventy years. Qualitative evidence, however, is clearly at odds with this hypothesis. Most economic historians would agree with Fowke's suggestion that 1930 marked "the end of the establishment phase of the wheat economy and the completion of the first national policy"[18] and would even go farther by using 1930 to mark the end of the period of extensive growth that started in Canada in the mid 1890s. By this time the West had been settled, the railways built, and the pulp and paper, hydroelectric, and mining industries established.[19] It is true that since the Second World War there have been some dramatic new mining developments in Canada—petroleum, iron ore, uranium, and potash—but the industries built on these new resources have been neither land-intensive nor labour-intensive and they have had a much smaller impact on the postwar economy than the earlier "staple industries" had on the pre-1930 economy. In retrospect, there seems as much reason to have expected some retardation in the growth of GNP in Canada after 1930 as there was to expect a slowing down of the GNP growth rate in the United States after 1900, that is to say, for a replacement of predominantly extensive growth by predominantly intensive growth.

Yet our growth statistics are still those of a period of extensive growth. In part, the statistics reflect the postwar resource discoveries, mentioned above, and in part, I think, the likelihood that the expansion in manufacturing in Canada after 1940 was unusually large not only because of the war but also because normal growth had been suspended in the 1930s. In a sense, those technological trends that were differentially favourable to Canadian manufacturing, discussed in chapter 4, had just begun to take hold in the 1920s, were submerged by the depression of the 1930s, and only became fully apparent in the 1940s and 1950s. But when this has been said, there still remains a strong suspicion that Canadian

[18]"The National Policy—Old and New" in the *Canadian Journal of Economics and Political Science*, August, 1952, pp. 277–8.
[19]See J. H. Dales, *Hydroelectricity and Industrial Development* (Cambridge, Mass., 1957), chap. 8, esp. p. 166.

*policy* has had much to do with the perpetuation of very high GNP growth rates characteristic of a period of extensive growth long after our period of extensive growth apparently came to an end.

The change in "national policies" after 1930 was not, perhaps, as sharp as Fowke suggested.[20] Indeed two out of three of the main pillars of the old national policy—tariff protection and the promotion of immigration—are as much a feature of present-day Canadian policy as they were of Canadian policy sixty years ago. As has been argued throughout this book the Canadian tariff and Canadian immigration policy operate jointly to "force the pace" of manufacturing growth, and, more generally, of growth in population and GNP. The danger is that in a period of intensive growth, when the growth in natural resources is slower than the growth in population, part of the growth in GNP will be at the expense of growth in GNP per person. American adjustments to the "closing" of their "frontier" included, one might suggest, a rapid extension of birth control practices, severe limitations on immigration, land conservation policies, and, more recently, growing concern for the wise use of air and water. Some of these adjustments have also been in evidence in Canada. But our *national* economic policies today are substantially those of 1900—more factories, more people, more cities, more GNP. Is it not time to consider whether these are appropriate policies for a country whose "frontier" was "closed" a generation ago?

[20]"The National Policy—Old and New."

# 8

## On Size and Scale

It will by now have become obvious—perhaps oppressively so—that the main argument of this book is that the Canadian tariff tends continuously to increase the *size* of the Canadian population and the Canadian economy (GNP) while at the same time reducing the *quality* of Canadian economic life (GNP per capita). Yet in the *Second Annual Review* of the Economic Council of Canada, it is asserted on page 52 that "Population expansion appears to have been a positive factor encouraging long-run growth of real income per person in both countries [Canada and the United States]."

Both my statement and the Council's are made subject to the assumption that other things, including technological change, are held constant; within that assumption, the Council says that an increased population "appears to" increase real income per person, while I say that increased population will reduce real income per person. One of us must be wrong! The opposite views derive from vastly different evaluations of the validity for Canada of arguments from "the economies of scale." The Council thinks economies of scale are very significant; I think they are so insignificant that they can be safely ignored. Indeed, I think that in most cases it is dangerous for policy-makers to heed their siren-like song. The disagreement raises issues of both theory and fact.

# I

Let us begin with fundamentals. The claim of economics to be a science rests basically on its conception of an "optimum" or "equilibrium" size for the magnitudes it studies—whether it be the amount of labour hired by a firm or the amount of money a household spends on chewing gum. An equilibrium quantity is one that is neither too large nor too small, and the criterion for such a quantity is that some *average* magnitude —such as utility per dollar spent, value of output per dollar's worth of input, or income per person—shall be maximized.

Arguments from economies of scale contend that the greater the absolute *size* of a unit the greater will be its *efficiency*; for each size of unit there will be an optimum disposition of its resources that maximizes its "rate of return," but the larger-sized unit will always enjoy a *higher* rate of return at *its* optimum than a smaller-sized unit will at *its* optimum. If economies of scale always applied—and none of their proponents argues that they *always* apply—a larger household would always be able to obtain more satisfaction for a dollar's worth of expenditure than a smaller household; a larger firm would always be more profitable than a smaller firm; a larger industry would always be able to produce at lower costs than a smaller industry; and a larger economy would always yield a higher standard of living than a smaller economy. If this sort of argument were not restrained it is clear that the whole *science* of economics would quickly degenerate into the vulgar maxim, "the bigger the better." Economists spend most of their time arguing that nothing in this world is free; yet often, near the end of the lecture, they relent and suggest that there may be a Santa Claus after all. For the "economies of scale" is at bottom a Santa Claus argument; it says that if you double your inputs you may reap more than double the output, and thereby get something for nothing.

Popular belief in the argument derives, I think, from the common observation that a plant *of given size* can increase its profitability by increasing the *size of its output* and thereby

160

"spreading its overhead" over more units of output. Even if this proposition were true (and it is not true in all situations) it would have nothing to do with economies of scale; the increased profits are said to arise as a result of increased output from a plant of *given size,* and nothing is said about the probable profits to be derived from increased output produced in a *larger* plant. Confusion between "size of output" and "size of plant" is apt to arise in popular literature, but the two are seldom confused in the professional literature. Indeed the main presumption in economics is that plants will be built at an optimum size to begin with; optimum size may change over time, but plants built in any given year will be built at a size that will incorporate all scale economies that are then known. The only exception to this rule will occur when the prospective demand (both domestic and foreign) for the firm's output is less than its optimum output. The firm will then build an "under-sized" plant, or build an optimum-sized plant and "under-utilize" it. When the exception applies, there will be only one firm in the industry. Thus whenever the market served by an industry is large enough to absorb the output of more than one optimum-sized plant, we may be sure that, whatever the ills the industry may suffer from, the inability to achieve "economies of scale" because of "too small a market" is not one of them. Common observation suggests that there are few, if any, industries in Canada where the size of the available market is so small that it precludes production at an optimum scale; the case studies of several industries made recently by H. E. English lead to the same conclusion.[1]

Thus, whatever the popular appeal of an "infant industry" argument for tariffs based on the economies of scale *as these relate to the individual firm or plant,* the argument has no scientific validity, and never has had any validity. If the available market is large enough to support an optimum-sized plant built in a particular location the plant will be built without public aid in the form of tariff protection; if the available market is not this large it can most efficiently be served

[1]H. E. English, *Industrial Structure in Canada's International Competitive Position* (Canadian Trade Committee, 1964).

161

by existing optimum-sized plants located elsewhere. Firms do not "grow" to optimum size; they are born that way. Tariff protection can ensure the survival of an under-sized or poorly located firm; but it cannot make the firm "grow" to optimum size, or change a high-cost location into a low-cost location.

Scientific arguments based on economies of scale therefore refer to "external" economies, advantages that accrue to firms *of a given size* as the result either of an increase in the size of the *industry* (i.e., an increase in the number of firms of a given size in the industry), or of an increase in the size of the whole economy. The former type of scale economies may be called "industry-wide economies," and the latter "economy-wide economies." It is possible to construct an infant industry argument based on these economies, but it is not a very convincing one. It should be noted, too, that the argument is stronger in my model, where protection *does* increase GNP, and therefore the size of the economy and the size of the industries composing it, than in the conventional model where protection *reduces* GNP and thus reduces the possible level of economy-wide economies even though it may increase the level of possible industry-wide economies in some industries.

Although industry-wide economies no doubt exist, so do industry-wide diseconomies. There is no evidence I know of that in Canada today the former outweigh the latter; indeed, growing problems of air and water pollution and traffic congestion might reasonably suggest that further increase in industry size would result in a net balance of industry-wide diseconomies. In any event, in the present state of our knowledge, I can see no justification for basing public policy decisions on the assumption that the reverse is true.

Economy-wide economies are subject to all the doubts surrounding industry-wide economies, for an economy is, after all, the sum of its industries. However, the economy-wide argument has one merit that the industry-wide argument does not have. Social overhead capital for an economy—particularly such things as transport systems, communications systems, and power networks—may well have to be provided on a large scale or not at all. They are likely to be under-

162

utilized by a small economy; thus as an economy grows the services of such social capital (an important part of the costs of all firms in the economy) can be provided at a lower cost per unit of service. How large does an economy have to be to make optimum use of its social capital? Is the Canadian economy large enough to use its social overhead capital efficiently?

I do not think there is convincing evidence to support either an affirmative or negative answer to the latter question. In the past, no doubt, the Canadian economy has gained economy-wide economies as a result of growth in its size. As was noted previously, and the Economic Council agrees,[2] this factor should have tended to close the income gap between Canadians and Americans. One might argue that the tariff, by increasing Canadian GNP, has made more economy-wide economies available to Canadians; but since the gap in incomes has in fact not tended to narrow this favourable effect of the tariff must have been more than offset by the unfavourable effects of protection. But let us ignore the past; today the answer to our question must surely remain a matter of opinion.

At least we have now arrived at a possible explanation of the difference of opinion noted at the beginning of this essay. The Economic Council could support its assertion by the view that further growth would provide Canadians with very large economy-wide economies. My own view is that even by the end of the Second World War the Canadian economy was large enough to make efficient use of its social capital, and that therefore future growth, unless justified by technological change, is likely to yield as many economy-wide diseconomies as economies.

## II

The question of a country's "optimum" population, the population that would maximize income per capita in the country,

2*Second Annual Review* (Ottawa, 1966), p. 52.

used to be actively discussed in economics. The supposition was that, in a given state of technology, there was some combination of mobile resources (people and capital) on the one hand and immobile natural resources on the other that would yield the maximum income per capita; income per capita would be smaller if the population were either smaller or larger than the "optimum." The theory fell out of fashion because it was presented at such a high level of abstraction, in terms of the immeasurables of "technology" and "resources," that it was quite impossible to specify, even roughly, what a country's optimum population was likely to be at any given time. The optimum population was a non-operational concept if there ever was one; and I can see no way of making it operational. What is important to realize, however, is that public policy may often be based on a presumed answer to a non-operational question.

In Canada, it seems to me, there is, and always has been, some sort of a consensus that the country is woefully underpopulated. The only economic test of underpopulation or overpopulation is, of course, income per capita; and every country in the world, except the one with the highest and the one with the lowest standard of living, is underpopulated with respect to countries with a lower standard of living and overpopulated with respect to countries with a higher standard of living. Canada is thus overpopulated with respect to the United States—considerably so, to judge from the size of the income gap between the two countries. Yet we still consider ourselves underpopulated relative to the United States. Why?

One of the most fatuous preconceptions of Canadians, especially Canadian politicians, is that we are "rich in natural resources." Relative to the United States this is simply not so; in the resources that count most in terms of their ability to support a large population—agricultural resources, coal and iron ore—we are a very small country by comparison with the United States. The resource situation is clearly reflected in the chart presented in chapter 6; our agricultural output is no more than 8 per cent of American agricultural output, and our manufacturing less than 8 per cent of American manufacturing output. Yet our population has been greater than 8 per cent of the United States population ever since 1920, and is now almost 10 per cent of the United States population. To me, these percentages suggest clearly that (1) Canada is *not* rich in natural resources relative to the United States and (2) that Canada is clearly overpopulated relative to the United States. On what grounds can it reasonably "appear" to the Economic Council of Canada that population growth *per se* is a "positive" factor tending to produce an increase in real income per capita in Canada?

Technology, no doubt, will continue to increase the population that Canada can support at the present, and even, probably, a higher standard of living. If technology increases the population that Canada can support (at the desired rate of increase in the standard of living) at a rate that is higher than the rate of natural population increase, net immigration in an amount sufficient to make up the difference in these rates is greatly to be desired on both economic and moral grounds. If there is no difference between these rates net immigration is undesirable on purely economic grounds—though gross immigration would be positive so long as there is gross emigration. I have no stomach for arguing the moral implications of immigration restrictions. Let me simply say that I see no moral reason for any immigration restriction anywhere; that everyone is aware of man's inhumanity to man; that I am writing a book on economics, that is to say, on a partial—but not for that reason an unimportant—view of the human comedy; and, finally, that it is by no means clear that in a world of poverty and immigration restrictions Canadians are making their maximum contribution to the solution of the poverty problem by pursuing a relatively "liberal" immigration policy (which, in the past at least, has been "liberal" only as to the amount of immigration, not as to its racial origin) on the one hand and a niggardly foreign aid policy on the other.

To return to the Canadian-American comparison that seems to obsess Canadians, it should be noted that the United States consciously *reduced* the prospective levels of its GNP growth rate in the early 1920s by its immigration restrictions. We on the other hand, to judge by our official policies, still hunger after higher and higher population growth rates and GNP growth rates. The common claim that we do so *in order to increase our standard of living* at once gives the lie to the frequently associated claim that our immigration policy is based on high moral considerations and displays an utter disregard for the intricacies of the optimum population problem. In my opinion the pressure for a Big Canada that is exerted by politicians, big business, and a large segment of the general population, represents a vulgar wish for bigness for its own sake. In this volume I have tried to argue that the Canadian tariff is one of the results of a desire for bigness for its own sake, that it conduces to this end, and that the main cost of its success in this respect has been a deterioration in the quality of the economic—and even the non-economic—life of Canadians.

# Index

Automotive Agreement, Canada–United States, 23–8

Bhagwati, J., 11n, 93n

Canadian–American historical comparison: similarities, 82–3; differences, 83–4; difference in protection, 80–2; "resource" difference, 84–7; "immigration" difference, 87–9; technique of, 82–3. *See also* "Time series of percentages"

Canadian–American income differential: stability of, 2, 84, 116, 119, 130n; and demography, 87–9, 117–20; and protection, 121–2, 123–5; "unexplained difference" in, 122–3; historically, 126–7, 129–30

Canadian tariff policy; historical interpretation of, 108–9, 147–9; previous studies of, 108–10; author's views on, 1, 3, 127, 129, 159, 166. *See also* National (developmental) policies

Comparative advantage: 11–28, 31–2; "classical" view, 12–13, 21; "modern" view, 13–14, 21; test for, 92–100

Comparative history: 6, 78–80, 89–90; holds "time" constant, 83, 90. *See also* Canadian–American historical comparison

Constant tariff: 5, 49–72, 116n; defined, 55–6; and increase in demand, 58–60, 64–5; and decrease in costs, 60–3, 65–7; and trends in money wages, 69–70; and balance of payments equilibrium, 68–72. *See also* Protection, Protected sector

Economic Council of Canada, 2, 8, 96n, 123n, 159, 163, 165

Economic history and economic theory, 7–8, 49–50, 154–5

"Economies of scale": 89, 109, 115n, 159; distinguished from optimum size of plant, 160–2; equated to external economies, 162–3

Effective protection: defined, 29; American tariff argued to be ineffective, 6–7, 34n, 80, 92, 104; test for, in Canada, 81, 91–92, 100–105. *See also* Protection

Extensive and intensive growth, 154–8

Factor-price equalization theorem, 25–7, 30

Factor proportions, 13–15, 18

GNP, *see* National income

Immigration: 117–18; policies in Canada and the United States, 4, 34n, 87–9, 119, 158, 165; and excess demand for labour in Canada, 119–22. *See also* Migration function

Immobility assumption. *See* Ricardian assumption

Infant industry argument, 50, 56–7, 109–10, 143, 161–2

"Innis link" of tariffs & railways, 145–7, 151–2

Location theory, 3, 18, 23, 26, 27

MacDougall, G. D. A., 93n

Manufacturing, primary and secondary: definition, 133; trends in, 113–14, 127–8, 130, 133, 135

Migration function, 3–4, 17–18, 34, 36–7, 53, 53n, 117–18

Mobility of factors: differential, 3, 15–19, 22, 30–1; and domestic trade, 3, 20, 23. *See also* Migration function

National (developmental) policies: promoted by Sir John A. Macdonald, 144–5; inconsistencies in 148–50; comment on, 150–4. *See also* Canadian tariff policy

167

National income, total and per capita figures: as indicators of extensive *v.* intensive growth, 7, 155–8, and of quantity *v,* quality of economic life, 48, 144, 166; identical movements of, when factor supplies fixed, 53, and different movements of, when factor supplies variable, 54; divergent movements of, 37, 41, 116, 120, 127, 130–1, 159; divergences of, with a constant tariff, 60, 62–3, 65, 66, 67, 116n; "shift" effects and the total figure, 54n, 72–3, 115

National Policy. *See* Canadian tariff policy

Ohlin, B., 20n

Optimum population: 163–4; Canada overpopulated relative to United States, 165

Parker, W. N., 78–9

Population growth in Canada, 116–19, 129–30

Protected sector: equilibrium size of, 42, 67–8, 71–2; and "wage parity," 122; growth of, 113, 129. *See also* Protection, Constant tariff

Protection, amount of: defined, 51; effects on growth rates, 54–5

burden of: defined, 51; long-run effects of, 45–8, 129

rate of: defined, 51; and tariff rates, 49, 80, 91

effects on: income, total and per capita, 37, 41; external value

of currency, 38, 71; rate of interest 37–9, 40n; natural resource rents, 39–40; factor supplies and prices, 35–43; character of population, 43–5, 47; domestic capital supply, 48; money wages, 105–7. *See also* Constant tariff, Protected sector, Effective protection

Ricardian assumption: 3, 12–13, 16, 18, 29–30, 36, 45; rejected by modern governments, 21–2

"Rule of Two," 15, 18–19, 28

Salter, W. E. G., 5, 47, 72n, 97n, 125

Technology: assumption concerning, 51n, 93; and natural resources, 33, 85–6; differential effects of, 51n, 85, 127–8

"Time series of percentages": 82–3, 92, 111–12, 131; productivity and wages, 101–6; output, income, population, 112–25; for period since 1870, 125–9

Timlin, Mabel F., 40n

Trade theory: various possible models, 19; desirability of extension to include factor movements, 3, 15, 18, 23; lack of theory of domestic trade, 3, 20; policy implications of different assumptions, 21–3; and division of labour, 28. *See also* Location theory

Young, J. H., estimate of "cash cost" of Canadian tariff, 46n, 102, 102n, 107, 110, 124–5

168